The Cutbush Connections:
In Flowers,
In blood
And in the Ripper case.

By Amanda Harvey Purse

Forget me not...

Published in 2018 by FeedARead.com Publishing

Copyright © The author as named on the book cover.

The author or authors assert their moral right under the Copyright, Designs and Patents Act, 1988, to be identified as the author or authors of this work.

All Rights reserved. No part of this publication may be reproduced, copied, stored in a retrieval system, or transmitted, in any form or by any means, without the prior written consent of the copyright holder, nor be otherwise circulated in any form of binding or cover other than that in which it is published and without a similar condition being imposed on the subsequent purchaser.

A CIP catalogue record for this title is available from the British Library.

Other works by the same author

Fictional

Jack the Ripper's Many Faces

Dead Bodies Do Tell Tales

The Strange Case of Caroline Maxwell

The Adventures of Amelia Christie

Binky the Tabby Cat tales

Factual

Jack and Old Jewry: The City of London Policeman Who Hunted the Ripper

Inspector Reid: The Real Ripper Street

E – Book

Victorian Lives behind Victorian Crimes series

Foreword

The reason I decided to write a full book on Charles Henry Cutbush was not only because he was a policeman that had some involvement in the Jack the Ripper case.

Much like my previous book, Inspector Reid: The Real Ripper Street, I was writing another book when Charles Henry briefly popped up, on my radar and the more I researched him, the more I realised he was another policeman that could not be defined in a chapter alone[1].

There was so much to write about and I felt that the man behind the career needed to be expressed fully in a book, as his suggested connections to a Jack the Ripper suspect and perhaps his sudden death could be thought of as over shadowing him a little.

There is always a life before a death and in this book, I hope to produce a fuller, perhaps detailed picture of Charles Henry.

To do this, I have not just focus of Charles Henry's immediate family, as sometimes we can gather

---

[1] The author would also like to point out here that, the reader may notice there is no official chapters within this book. That is because, the author wanted the story of the Cutbush family to flow continuously, not to stop and start. However, the author understands that this book may not be able to read in one go, so there are breaks within it.

more information and discover events that may have shaped the person, we are researching, through their grandparent's lives, which in turn may have shaped their parents lives and then onto the actual person we are concentrating on.

With Charles Henry we, as researchers, are lucky to be able to trace his family back to the 1720's, and from there his family tree was very vast, opening us up to meeting various interesting characters along the way.

These interesting characters have, as we can imagine, interesting tales to tell of themselves and it is extraordinary how much history seemed to repeat itself with Charles Henry in a number of different ways.

So, without looking into the Cutbush family tree, we could have missed so much of the background of this Victorian policeman.

I have been wonderfully honoured to have been in contact with various members of the Cutbush family tree and have seen family photographs of some of the key people within Charles Henry's life, which I have described at the end of the book.

To actually have seen what these people had looked like, to see what Charles Henry would have seen through his own eyes and *indeed a mirror*, has given me a different look on the life of this policeman.

I hope to share this different look with you, the reader, as we discover more about this man together.

I hope that we discover Charles Henry as a baby, being carried into church. A young boy having to grow up fast after, sadly, the death of a few family members. I hope we discover the young man taking on responsibilities that may not have been his own at the time and having to take the brave step in moving to London, starting a brand-new career, marrying and having children of his own.

Of course, being a policeman, there are cases and events to write of within his career. However, I hope to not just write of these facts, but to think of what the facts may mean and whether this could tell us anything of the man, himself.

The suggestions within this book are just that, suggestions. I could even state that they may not always be my own suggestions, but suggestions that may have been thought of by anyone, reading this, as events happen within this book.

I would never wish to force any of these suggestions on to you as we do not always think the same, do we?

The suggestions purely within this book are to be used as examples of what we can ask, what we maybe thinking, what we can question, if we look at events in a perhaps a slightly different, open minded way.

Examples of what we may notice if we think a little outside of the box and though these suggestions whether we can actually get to know Charles Henry after so much time has passed between us.

Suggestions do not always lead to an open door however, researching those suggestions is never easy and can often lead to a blocked wall.

I have not dismissed this fact and as I want the reader the feel that they are with me on this project, every step of the way, I often show the blocked walls.

My reasoning for this is that I want to show the possible workings out of why we have ended up with the suggestions or events we have in a person's life.

Hopefully this will make the whole project more real to the reader as their important input in this can never be denied.

I hope, as we are researching Charles Henry Cutbush, together, we can at least come close to get to know him.

That we might be able to picture the human being behind the name, 130 years after that name was ever attached to the Jack the Ripper case in whatever form. Finally, I hope this book does him proud.

Amanda Harvey Purse
Author
2018

Acknowledgements

The author has to thank so many people that have kindly helped along the way, if she misses anyone out she wholeheartedly apologises.

As an added bonus to this book which is about family connections, the author would like to thank her own family, who have got involved within this book in many different ways, they all know who they are and what they have done. I truly thank you all.

The author would like to thank, Cathy at St Nicholas Church, Sandhurst, Royal Masonic Girls School and London Orphans School. Paul and all the staff at Highgate Cemetery, Beth at Linda's Florist, Ashford. Judde House School, Tonbridge School, Imperial War Museum, Level Crossing Cemetery and Freemason Hall Museum.

The Canterbury Cathedral Archives, Terry at Canterbury City Cemetery. War Graves, Sliver Badge, Surrey Archives, Croydon Museum, Ashford Museum, Stockwell College, The National Archives and The Metropolitan Police Heritage Centre.

The author would like to thank all family members of the vast tree belonging to the surname of Cutbush, that she has been in contact with. The author is very much indebted to you all for many different reasons, which will all be explained in the book.

Finally, the author would like to thank Charles Henry Cutbush. There is always a reason why the author feels she has to write a full book of a peculiar policeman, she doesn't do it on a whim and she doesn't it to 'just write another book'.

There are certainly many personal reasons why the author feels very close to the Cutbush family story in all manner of its different levels.

However, she never knew quite how close she was to the history of this family until Charles Henry popped up on her radar and she can't help but thank him for all his story has shown her.

Introduction

Charles Henry Cutbush joined the Metropolitan Police force in the 1860's, he worked his way up to being a Superintendent of the Executive Branch of Scotland Yard, retiring in 1891.

Stating this, in this basic form can make us wonder why he is the central character within this book. However, one of the key reasons why his name might be known to you, comes in when we look at the dates in which he worked for the police force in London, 1860's to 1891.

In between these dates was the year of 1888. This was the year that the Great Blizzard hit the north-eastern side of America, by the end of which over four hundred people were to die. It was the year, that the last German Emperor and King of Prussia, Wilhelm II started to rule with a new policy for his Empire. This policy could be said to have led to a crisis after the assassination of Franz Ferdinand, which then led to the start of World War One.

It was the year that the African – American Frederick Douglass was first nominated to be American's president and was the year that Vincent van Gogh was said to have cut off his ear after a disagreement with fellow painter Paul Gauguin, of which he later was said to have sent his ear to a prostitute to keep safe.

In literature circles, 1888 would be the year that the English novelist and poet Thomas Hardy published his 'Wessex Tales', in which he writes about the restrictions of marriage, the problems of social rank and women's position in the 19th Century.

Robert Louis Stevenson's story The Black Arrow: A Tale of Two Roses was first published in full book form in this year. This was the story of Richard Shelton, that becomes a knight in the War of the Roses and who wants justice for the murder of his own father while falling in love with Lady Joanna Sedley.

Also in the May of 1888, Oscar Wilde writes his children's tales, which he groups under the title of The Happy Prince and other stories.

It would also seem to have been a very busy year for Sherlock Holmes[2]. As not only does Dr Watson 'recall' that Sherlock Holmes was working on the case called Valley of Fear in this year but he was also working on the adventures of A Scandal in Bohemia, Yellow Face, Greek Interpreter, Sign of Four and Hound of the Baskervilles. *A busy detective indeed...*

However, perhaps more importantly for a policeman working in London, 1888 was the year

---

[2] Written by Sir Arthur Conan Doyle.

a certain killer was roaming the streets of Whitechapel and the City of London.

This killer is still as famous now as they were then, when they were active. The name haunts like a spirit, the name sells in whatever form and yet funny enough, we don't actually know the real name of this killer...

However, through all the suspects there are out there, they all come together under the three little words of 'Jack the Ripper'.

Being a policeman within this time can make anyone seem famous for being just that, but some names might stick out in our minds more than others and we may not instantly think of Charles Henry Cutbush within this subject.

If we dig a little deeper into the name, we may find that there are many opinions on him and because of these opinions Charles Henry may seem at least, to have a stronger linkage to the Ripper case without him, even trying.

However, is the Jack the Ripper case the be all and end all to a Victorian policeman?

What about the man, the son, the father that stands behind the career?

Should we not try our best to discover Charles Henry, for him to be more a fuller, rounded person than a name, written on a report that because of its contents, has stood the test of time?

Well let's see what together, we can do and what we can possibly come up with...

Charles Henry Cutbush
1844 – 1896

The problems we have when researching Charles Henry's family tree is that to start with, there may seem to be a lot of Cutbush's in areas that could fit in well with what we know of Charles Henry's childhood and older life.

Also, they tend to have similar first and middle names, which makes learning the dates in which certain people are born even more important to get the right generation level on the family tree.

We also have an added pressure when mentioning this peculiar policeman's family. A pressure that is perhaps so great that it should be mentioned from the start.

This is because Charles Henry's connection to the Jack the Ripper case of 1888 has been suggested as not just adding his name to a report.

Charles Henry has been suggested as being a relation to Thomas Cutbush, who, as well as being a perpetrator of at least two stabbings in the capital of London, has been suggested as being the man behind the mysterious names of either 'The Whitechapel Murderer' or perhaps the better-known name of 'Jack the Ripper'.

This suggestion, if we take it back to the beginning, had its origins from a newspaper article in 1890's. The Sun newspaper ran a series of articles from their own research and a policeman's suggestion that Thomas Cutbush, who had wounded Florence Grace Johnson and Isabella Fraser in Kennington, London, had been sentenced and been classed to be insane in 1891, was also the murderer, Jack the Ripper.

These articles prompted a report by Sir Melville Macnaghten[3], the man that would be[4] the Assistant (Crime) Commissioner of the Metropolitan Police force.

This report, is known as The Macnaghten Memoranda and the main aim of it was to *disprove* Thomas Cutbush being a suspect, pointing to three other men that would fit the profile of being Jack the Ripper *more* in this policeman's eyes. These being Mr. M.J. Druitt, Kosminski and Michael Ostrog.

To explain this, Sir Melvin begins but detailing the information gathered on the Thomas Cutbush case, for example where Thomas was living, who he was living with, his career and why it was thought that Thomas was 'insane'.

---

[3] Born on the 16th June 1853 in London – Birth Record. Passing away on 12th May 1921 – Death Record.
[4] In 1903.

Melville Macnaghton, who would be the Assistant (Crime) Commissioner of the Metropolitan Police from 1903. He wrote a report disagreeing that Thomas Cutbush was Jack the Ripper.

However, the reason we have to mention this report is because of the nine little words, Sir Melville uses, almost as an 'off the cuff' statement at the end of his description of Thomas Cutbush.

He states, 'Cutbush was the nephew of the late Supt. Executive'.

Such a small and simple sentence, don't you think?

However, it is a sentence that has mystified many a researcher from that moment until now.

Could it really be possible that a Jack the Ripper suspect was related to a policeman that had some involvement into the investigation of that said crime?

What would this mean? What would this explain?

It could be easy to allow our minds to run away with many thoughts on this, however we have also got to play fair with this subject and although a policeman may have stated that Thomas Cutbush was related to Charles Henry, does that statement alone, make it true?

Should we not then investigate ourselves into this matter to find out if this was the case?

This open mindedness, has then got to make us question, what if Thomas Cutbush was not related to Charles Henry Cutbush?

Why would a policeman believe this was correct to mention it in his report?

Was he simply going on the same surname or did a piece of information get passed to this policeman which is unknown to us modern day researchers today?

Of course, much research into Thomas Cutbush's family tree has been made because of these questions, including perhaps getting a little confused over Kennington in London and Kennington in Kent.

However, this book is not to write of a Jack the Ripper suspect, there are and will be many books on that side of the case.

This book is about the policeman that had some involvement of the investigation of the murderous crimes of 1888, so instead of following Thomas Cutbush's family tree, in this book we will turn to Charles Henry's quite vast family tree.

Hopefully learning how interesting that tree is, how intriguing certain personalities were within it and perhaps how important it is to follow the correct Cutbush family, which is not always easy to do, but let us try.

The Roots of the Cutbush Family Tree
– The Sandhurst Connection

When tracing a family tree of a person you are researching you can never be sure how far back in time you are going to go with the family at the beginning of your research.

Wonderfully, with Charles Henry's family tree we can travel back to the 1720's, with the birth of William Cutbush and Elizabeth Martayne (sometimes wrote as Martin)[5].

These two people were both born in Sandhurst, Cranbrook in Kent, perhaps seeing each other every day and getting to know one another, they married in the same town on the 14th May 1741[6], both being in their twenties at the time.

These two people would be Charles Henry's Great Great Grandparents.

William[7] and Elizabeth[8] would go on to have two children, the youngest being Hannah Cutbush born about 1763[9], she has one child to whom she names John Cutbush[10] and he marries a Hannah Fowle on the 5th May 1788 in the church of St Nicholas, Sandhurst.[11]

---

5 Birth records.
6 Marriage records of the parish.
7 Who passes away on the 20th November 1791 and was buried at St Nicholas Church in Sandhurst on 26th November 1791– Death and Burial Records.
8 Who passed away on the 25th May 1777 and was buried at St Nicholas Church in Sandhurst on the 31st May 1777 – Death and Burial Records.
9 Birth records of the parish.
10 Father unknown – Birth Record.
11 Marriage Record. The couple then go on to have two children themselves, Hannah Cutbush b. 15th January 1791 and Anne

However, to follow the family tree of Charles Henry, we need to focus on William and Elizabeth's first born.

...

His name was John Cutbush, being born on 25th June 1752, in the town of Sandhurst, Cranbrook in Kent, just like his parents[12].

Quite oddly, John Cutbush was baptised at the church of St Nicholas on the 9th November 1796 at the age of forty four years old[13]. One can only wonder why John had decided to be baptised then, so late in his life. Was he ill at this time and not thought to survive?

If this was the case, he did recover to live for many more years. So, we may question if his wife was religious and if so she may have wanted him to do it?

A more reasonable suggestion to this occurrence comes in, when we look at the dates in which John's children were baptised.

We find *another* John Cutbush, born on the 2nd September 1796[14], he was to be the last child John Sr was to have and he was baptised on the 6th November 1796, just three days before his own father.

Can we then imagine conversations John Sr might have had, with the thought that John Junior being his eighth

---

Cutbush b.1796 – Birth Records.
12 Birth Certificate.
13 Baptism records of the parish.
14 Birth records of the parish.

child, being baptised and his father wasn't, to then decide to have himself baptised soon after? A reasonable suggestion if anything else.

John Sr marries Ann Couchman (born on 30th May 1755 in Sandhurst, Cranbrook in Kent[15]) on the 17th September 1779 in the same church John later becomes baptised in, St Nicholas in Sandhurst.

Sadly, in the grounds of this same church would also be where John's wife, Ann, would be buried on 5th September 1813, aged just fifty eight years old[16].

…

St Nicholas Church in Sandhurst was and still is today a very quaint Kentish village church with lovely stone built walls, wooden porches and strong dark wooden doors that must have seen many a person enter over the many years they have stood attached to the church.

The floor is of worn down stone, with red and black tiles that we can easy imagine have had many a foot placed on them. The brown wooden pews, each with a cross craved into their ends, sit there, posed for the action of being sat on and waiting for the familiar creek sound they produce when this action is completed.

However, the two things that struck the author the most when she visited the church was firstly, the way the headstones that, surround all four sides of this church, had been managed to be both beautifully maintained, (so much

---

15 Birth and Death records of the parish.
16 Birth and Death records of the parish.

so that every headstone that has survived over the years, can be not only seen but visited without much difficulty at all) plus it also manages to look like a pretty English garden.

With bluebells and buttercups growing around some of the last resting places of people that were once known in the area, almost as if Mother Nature was quietly hugging the souls that these places belonged to, in the most charming way.

The second thing the author noticed was that, with all the history that lays within the church's interior, one item, made of stone, connected the church to the reason why the author was visiting it.

That item was the *font,* where the family members, we could even say, *the roots of the Cutbush family*, (as without them, we researchers would not have had Charles Henry Cutbush to hopefully get to know in this book) were baptised.

...

John and Ann would have eight children together, James being born on the 9th December 1781[17], we will return to James later on in this book.

The next child John and Ann were to have was Charles being born on the 17th July 1783, who sadly dies in Cranbrook Workhouse in 1870, at the age of eighty eight years old[18].

---

17 Birth records.
18 Workhouse records.

He had become a Farm Labourer, working the fields in Kent, when he decided to marry his first wife, Mary Jeffery[19] on 10th August 1814[20]. However, Mary sadly passes away at the young age of nineteen, just a year after her marriage to Charles Cutbush, on 16th April 1815[21].

Charles then, remarries Mary Mummery on 1st November 1817 in the church of St Nicholas, Sandhurst[22].

They had six children together, John Cutbush, possibly named after Charles's father, born on 23rd October 1818[23], Hester Cutbush, born on 7th June 1820[24], Ann Cutbush born on 22nd February 1822[25], she like her father passes away in Cranbrook Workhouse[26].

---

19 Born in 1796 in Brenchley, Kent – Birth Record.
20 Marriage Record.
21 She is buried at St Nicholas Church in Sandhurst – Burial Record.
22 Parish Records.
23 Birth Record. He passes away in 1902, aged eighty three years old. – Death Record.
24 Birth Record. He passes away in 1898 aged seventy seven years old. - Death Record.
25 Birth Record.
26 Workhouse Records.

Author, both inside and outside of St Nicholas Church, Sandhurst.

Where relations of Charles Henry Cutbush were baptised, married and were buried.

The font were the early members of the Cutbush family were baptised in at St Nicholas Church.
©Amanda Harvey Purse.

The area which the early members of the Cutbush family are buried at St Nicholas Church.
©Amanda Harvey Purse.

The next child Charles and Mary[27] were to have was *William Cutbush[28] and this would be where the connection from Charles Henry Cutbush's family and the 'Tobacconist Cutbush's' comes in, which will be mentioned later in this book.*

...

As we have just seen two members of this side of the Cutbush family ended up in Cranbrook Workhouse and because these members also passed away inside of that workhouse, the author thought that she would visit the place.

Although the name of 'Cranbrook Workhouse' had moved around in the area, by the 1760's it was running from Sissinghurst Castle.

The Parliamentary Report closest to the time that both members of the Cutbush family were there, that the author could find to date, was dated 1777. In it, it shows that Cranbrook only held one hundred inmates.

This number might make us think that Cranbrook Workhouse was small in size if we were comparing it to images we may have in our heads of London workhouses.

However, when the nearby area of Benenden had only forty inmates at the time, Frittenden had also forty inmates and

---

27 Mary passed away on the 24th October 1834 at the age of fifty – Death Record.
28 William would have a younger sister, Caroline Cutbush b. 3rd December 1826 and a younger brother, James Cutbush b. 22nd September 1829 – Birth Records.

Goudhurst had fifty five inmates, for the locals at least, Cranbrook must have seemed to be quite large.

Sissinghurst Castle gardens are today run by the National Trust and is grade one listed. They have a quite large courtyard, containing of a few cottages and the Gatehouse that was used to house the inmates of the workhouse until 1855 when the buildings that were left, (the rest being pulled down) were used for the farm.

In the 1930's all that could be restored was The Gatehouse part and is still there today. It stands alone and quite prominent in the garden grounds.

As the author passed through the Gatehouse, all the images of the many inmates that must have worked hard in the Kentish Summer sun hit home for her.

Another thought came to the author as she looked up at the building, The Gatehouse, oddly reminded her of Hampton Court in London, if only in a condense version.

The reason for this was because of the style and the colour of the brickwork. The burned red colour of the bricks that built The Gatehouse and the two small turrets at the top, certainly give the building, a Tudor period appeal to the author.

Sissinghurst Castle today. Where two members of the Cutbush Family lived, worked and sadly passed away in, when it was Cranbrook Workhouse. ©Amanda Harvey Purse.

Author at Sissinghurst Castle.

Cutbush's Tobacconist Family Business

William was born on 15th July 1824[29] and by 1851 he was living with his first wife Sarah Wood and his daughter Mary, in Foston Green, Tenterden.

At this time, he was working on the fields of Kent, possibly working with his own father[30]. Sadly, the next few years was hard on William, firstly within a few months of her birth, William's daughter passes away[31]. Secondly, almost to the year of that death, in 1852, William's wife passes away[32].

We can imagine that, William may not have wanted to stay in Kent after the death of his wife and only child and we know by three years later William finds himself in the capital because in 1855, he remarries there.

He married Matilda Mary Horrell[33] in the first quarter of 1855 in St Pancras[34]. They had eight children together, Elizabeth Sarah Cutbush, born 1855 in St Pancras[35], Matilda Ellen Cutbush born 1858[36], William Cutbush born 1860[37], Caroline Cutbush born 1862[38], Charles Cutbush born 1864[39], Henry Cutbush born 1868[40], Thomas Cutbush

---

29 Birth Record.
30 1851 Census.
31 Death Record.
32 Death Record.
33 Born in 1831 in St Pancras – Birth Record.
34 Marriage Record.
35 Birth Record.
36 Birth Record.
37 Birth Record.
38 Birth Record.
39 Birth Record.

born 1870, who sadly died one year later[41] and finally, Edward Cutbush born 1872[42].

By 1861 this side of the Cutbush family was living at Number 11 High Street, in Highgate. This address was a Newsagents and Tobacconist, from which William worked, with a home for his family situated above the premises[43].

William continues to work in the high street until at least 1901 as he was mentioned on that years' census there and we can imagine being a Newsagents in the heart of the high street for well over forty years that William was well known within the area and the community.

In fact, a newspaper article states,

'Nearly fifty years ago he commenced business in Highgate as a newsagent and for many years he was almost the only agent in the neighbourhood... His genial nature made him a general favourite and his personal reminiscences of Highgate for so long a period were charmingly told and listened to with the greatest interest.'[44]

What is also interesting to note is that, with William and his family living in the High Street in Highgate, they were only a few minutes' walk away from another branch of the same Cutbush family mentioned later within this book.

William passes away on 18th March 1902[45]. His death was a sad one, but one that needs to be mentioned because of its connections to our policeman's history.

---

40 Birth Record.
41 Birth and Death Record.
42 Birth Record.
43 1861 Census.
44 15th March 1902 – Hampstead and Highgate Express.
45 Death Record.

William's health had been declining since an accident he had in 1900, in which he injured his right knee. This had cause him to be in great pain, he was also suffering from pain emotionally too, as it was around time that his wife had passed away and 'he felt her loss keenly'.[46]

What the newspaper journalist who wrote those lines probably did not know was that this was the second wife, William had lost.

William was quite young when he lost his first wife and child and we can never know how someone is feeling or how they are coping with such an event.

Everything could seem normal and William certainly seemed from the outside to have carried on with his life, running a business, remarrying and having more children. However mental illness can show itself in often shocking ways.

...

Edward Cutbush, William's son, had left his father on the Wednesday night in his shop, smoking his pipe. Edward was due to be back in the shop the next morning and on arrival, Edward knocked on the door but oddly, he got no answer.

Edward thought this was not right because he could see that the lights were on in the shop. So, Edward turned to a neighbour, a painter called John McMullin, for help getting

---

46 15th March 1902 – Hampstead and Highgate Express.

the door open and once inside, Edward went in search of his father.

He found that his father's bed had not been slept in, so he searched the other rooms and upon entering the kitchen, Edward sadly found his father.

William had hanged himself in the night by using a piece of cord nailed to the ceiling.

William had left a note but the handwriting was so bad that only a few words could be understood such as 'good boys' and 'broken hearted father'.[47]

We can only imagine what William must have been feeling when he decided to take his own life, similarly we do not know how his death affected the family.

Although, this occurrence is just as hard to write as it is for anyone to read, this had to be mentioned because, William was a relation to Charles Henry, so perhaps knowing the family background of this policeman will allow us to understand circumstances involving him later on, a little better, than we did before.

Sadly, the death toll for this side of the Cutbush family was to rise, as just six months after the shocking death of her father, Caroline Cutbush passes away and was buried on the 12th September 1902.

She was thirty nine years of age at the time of her passing and was described as having a 'genial and obliging' manner

---

47 17th March 1902 – Islington Daily Gazette and North London Tribune.

which made her a favourite in the area. She had been ill for some months previously and was buried in Highgate Cemetery[48].

We will soon find out she was not the only Cutbush in this family to have been buried there.

---

48 13th September 1902 – Hampstead and Highgate Express.

Back to
The Sandhurst Connection

William's Aunt, Mary was the third child to be born to John and Ann Cutbush, being born on the 21st November 1785 and who passed away on the 2nd March 1872, aged eighty six years old.

William Cutbush was next, possibly named after John's father, being born on 8th February 1788, passing away on the 27th January 1854 in Highgate, London (we will return to this William Cutbush later in the book).

Ann Cutbush, possibly named after her mother was born on 29th April 1790, Hannah, possibly named after John's sister, was born on 17th August 1792 and passes away in 1858 in Ashford, Kent, aged sixty five years old.

We will see later how the town of Ashford in Kent becomes important to the life of Charles Henry Cutbush and with mentioning this here we can see the beginnings of a connection the Cutbush family has to that town from this point on, with Hannah Cutbush ending her life there. *Hannah being Charles Henry's Great Aunt.*

Sarah Cutbush was to follow, being born on 11th April 1794 and as already mentioned in this book, John Cutbush Junior was born on the 2nd September 1796, passing away in 1884 in Harrietsham, Kent, aged eighty eight years old[49].

---

49 Birth and Death Records of the parishes.

Their father, John Sr would pass away within the same town that he was born and had worked in (once being a Miller's assistant) in 1841[50].

...

To continue Charles Henry's family tree down we would need to follow, the oldest child to John and Ann Cutbush, James.

However, the author would wish to take this moment to make a slight detour and mention other relations to Charles Henry here.

The reason the author wishes to do this, is because before we step down another level in the family linkage, there is a person that through his hard work made the name of Cutbush quite famous, even until the 1960's.

This comes in through James's brother, William, making him Charles Henry's Great Uncle.

---

50 Death Record of the parish.

The Cutbush and Sons Family Business

William, as mentioned before, was born on the 8th February 1788, he was baptised in the church of St Nicholas in Sandhurst, Kent on 16th March 1788[51].

He married Sarah Belton[52] (sometimes spelt with two 'l's') on 2nd October 1820 in the church of St Alphage in Greenwich[53]. Their first child, William Junior, is not easily found on records at first. What does not help in finding him is that his date of birth changes in the censuses.

This could have been a mistake on the records, as if you have research any family tree before, you will know mistakes like these do happen, often.

However, it is interesting to note that on this occasion, this child, was first recorded on the census as being born in 1816[54], four years before William and Sarah got married, he then is recorded as being born in the year of their marriage[55,56].

This can allow us to suggest that, maybe William Junior was born before the marriage and perhaps his year of birth was changed to fit in with the date of the marriage later on, as this was not an uncommon action to take at this period of

---

51 Birth and Baptism record of the parish.
52 Born in 1795 in Croydon – Birth Record.
53 Marriage Record.
54 1841 census.
55 As to date, William Junior's Birth Record has not been found to indicate which year he was actually born.
56 The later censuses.

time. However, without knowing the full circumstances of the family at this time, we cannot be sure.

William Junior married Mary Ann Broxup on 29th September 1840 in Enfield[57], Mary Ann was born in 1818 in Middlesex, London and on the 1841 census, they were living in the High Street in Barnet.

This address was very important to the Cutbush family as William Junior takes on a branch of the family business there, in Barnet.

...

The family business was owning a quite famous Florist and Nursery, which by 1905 would have a Royal Appointment from King Edward VII, allowing them to be the official providers of plants and flowers in the Royal Parks of London.

William's father had begun the business from his detached house at Number 40 Highgate West Hill. Before William Sr took over this building, it was originally two houses, Number 45, once owned by Mrs Bonser and Number 46, owned by Miss Parker[58].

The house was made into one, under one new number, Number 40 by Mr. Bowstreed, who ran a nursery from the premises[59].

---

57 Marriage Record.
[58] Survey of London in the Village of Highgate. The parish of St Pancras Part 1: Volume 17 (1836) by Percy Lovell and William McB Marcham.
[59] Survey of London in the Village of Highgate. The parish of St Pancras Part 1: Volume 17 (1836) by Percy Lovell and William

In fact, we can see the area of land the house was situated on, in a map of London dated 1804, in which it is described as 'Mr. Bowstreed's Nursery'. The numbers have since been changed again and the house is now situated at Number 80 Highgate West Hill[60] today.

This house was brought by William Sr in 1822, two years after his marriage to Sarah and he added to the house by 1834, proving that William had earned his craft to be able to afford to do this[61].

It had a Fish-scale and Diamond slate roof with carved gables and a tall brick chimney. It was two storeys high, with four windows, one of which was bay shaped. The seed shop and office were to the side of the house in a large conservatory.[62]

Although the conservatory no longer exists, the house still stands where this part of the Cutbush family once lived and worked from, for at least one hundred years[63], (before moving to be situated next to the old police station in

---

McB Marcham.
60 Survey of London in the Village of Highgate. The parish of St Pancras Part 1: Volume 17 (1836) by Percy Lovell and William McB Marcham.
61 Survey of London in the Village of Highgate. The parish of St Pancras Part 1: Volume 17 (1836) by Percy Lovell and William McB Marcham.
62 Survey of London in the Village of Highgate. The parish of St Pancras Part 1: Volume 17 (1836) by Percy Lovell and William McB Marcham.
63 Ending its days in 1918, possibly to coincide with the death of Herbert Cutbush, the then director of the business and William's grandson.

Highgate until the 1960's[64]) making it Grade Two listed and to date, worth nearly three million pounds[65].

At the time William added to the home, the family had grown in size. There was now James Cutbush, born in 1827, Emma Cutbush born 1829[66] and Reuben Cutbush born 1831[67][68].

Sadly, William Sr may not have seen the fruits of his labour flourish into the grand business, we know it to be later on as he passes away on 27th January 1854.

He was buried, like his relation mentioned before in this book, in Highgate Cemetery, which was situated very close to his house in West Hill[69].

His wife, Sarah, possibly out of grief, moves out of this address and goes to live with her oldest son, William Junior at the Barnet branch of the Cutbush and Sons business.

The address was in an area of Barnet called South Mimms and like his father before him, William and his family were living on the premises, where he worked.

William Junior did not just have his wife and his mother living with him by 1861, but he also had his niece[70], Sarah Cutbush, born 1856 and a servant called Eliza Lawrence[71].

---

64 The author would like to thank Del Purse here for this nugget of information, *of which he has plenty*.
65 Local estate agents pricing.
66 She passes away in the nearby area of Edmonton in 1892, at the age of sixty three years old – Death Record.
67 Birth Records.
68 He was baptised in the church of St Michael, Highgate, on 29th May 1831 – Baptism Record.
69 Death Record.

Sarah, William's mother, passes away within the same year of the 1861 census. So well-known was this side of the Cutbush family already, that Sarah's passing was recorded in The Illustrated London News, she had passed away on 6th September 1861, her age being recorded as of sixty one.[72]

...

William Jr meanwhile becomes a Freemason, being a part of the Gladsmuir Lodge Number 1385[73]. Sadly, William passes away rather suddenly in the second quarter of 1876[74], while on a seaside trip to Brighton in Sussex.

He passes away in a similar fashion to how his younger brother, James would do later on, with having an apoplectic fit[75].

His sudden death caused a few problems within the Cutbush family, because it seems as if William was in the motion of changing his Will at the time of his death.

His original Will divided his property in equal amounts to his wife, his brothers and sister, however William might have been discussing with his younger brother James, for him to take over the whole business in Barnet as James owned the Highgate and Finchley branches already.

---

70 The first child born to William's youngest brother, Reuben
71 1861 census.
72 14th September 1861 – Illustrated London News.
73 8th August 1885 – Freemason.
74 Death Record.
75 8th August 1885 – Freemason.

To overcome this problem, Mary Ann, William's widow decided to pass the business on to her brother in law, James, as William would have wanted, as long as James paid her a certain amount each year.

This was the agreement which everyone abided by, until three years later, when James failed pay up.

By 1883, James claimed bankruptcy, meaning that if accepted, he would not have pay any of his debts, including to his sister in law, William's widow.

This did not go down well with the family as we can imagine and it led to the courts taking stock owned by James to pay his debt.

However, James made the point that the court took stock that was worth more than what was owed and he was promised that goods would not be taken[76].

Although it seems as if James won his cause, this family dispute was all played out in the courts, something we imagine did not help family relations.

…

In the same year as William Sr death, there was a happy occasion for this part of the Cutbush family. William and Sarah's youngest child and *Charles Henry's Great cousin, Reuben* gets married on 21st November 1854 to Sarah Jane Hawkins[77] in the same church Reuben was baptised in, St Michael's Highgate.

---

76 24th March 1883 – The Barnet Press, Finchley News, and Edgware Chronicle.
77 Born on 10th October 1829 in Islington – Birth Record.

Reuben and Sarah Jane had eight children in total, Sarah Ann Cutbush[78], Charles William Reuben Cutbush[79], James Henry Cutbush[80], Eleanor Cutbush[81], William Cutbush[82], Lydia Mary Cutbush[83], Reuben Edwin Cutbush[84] and finally, Lionel Lea Cutbush[85].

---

78 Born 1855 in Edmonton – Birth Record. She marries Thomas Sherret Taylor in 1885 in Mile End – Marriage Record. They have four children together, Thomas Bruce Taylor in 1886 in Limehouse, Bernard Sherret Taylor in 1889 in Stepney, Dorothy Helen Taylor in 1893 in West Ham and Beryl Hope Taylor in 1897 West Ham – Birth Records. The author can follow this family line down further but we could be stepping too far from Charles Henry here.
79 Born 1857 in Islington – Birth Record. He becomes a Fish Salesman – census. He marries Harriet Jane Bunn in 1879 in Mile End – Marriage Record. They have five children together, Charles Albert Cutbush born in 1880, Ethel Harriet Cutbush born in 1882, Elsie Harriet Cutbush born in 1887, Ivy Helena Cutbush born in 1890 and Percy Edward Cutbush born in 1896 – Birth Records. Charles William Reuben Cutbush passed away on 20th January 1932 in Romford – Death Record.
80 Born in 1861 in Islington – Birth Record. Like his brother Charles, James becomes a Fish Saleman too – Census. He marries Helen Jarrett in 1900 in Hackney – Marriage Record. They have one child, born in the same year as their marriage in 1900, Henry Cutbush.
81 Born in 1863 in Holloway – Birth Record. She marries Sid Pritchard Sim in 1886 in Stepney – Marriage Record. They have two children together, Margaret Eleanor Sim born in 1886 in Mile End and Sidney Cutbush Sim born in 1887, who sadly died aged four in 1891 – Birth and Death Records.
82 Born in 1868 in Holloway – Birth Record. Like his brothers before him, he also becomes a Fish Salesman and Auctioneer – census. He marries Ellen Clara Sales in 1891 in Hackney – Marriage Record. They have three children together, William Charles Cutbush born on 5th November 1893 in Mile End, Charles Herbert Cutbush born in 1895 in Mile End and Ellen Louise Cutbush born in 1897 in Forest Gate – Birth Record.
83 Born in 1868 in Middlesex – Birth Record. She sadly passes away at the age of fourteen years old in 1882 – Death Record.
84 Born in 1870 in Stepney – Birth Record. He sadly passes away at

Reuben doesn't follow in the family business that his father, William had made, as he becomes an Oil and Colour Man[86].

Reuben Cutbush sadly passes away on 1st August 1901 and was buried in Manor Park Cemetery[87].

Reuben's older sister, Emma Cutbush, married Henry William Holden in the March of 1855[88].

They had four children together, Emma Jane Holden[89], Henry Alfred Holden[90], Mary Isabel Holden[91] and Frederick George Holden[92]. Emma passes away in 1892 in Edmonton[93].

---

the age of eleven years old in 1881 – Death Record.
85 Born in 1873 in Mile End – Birth Record. He becomes like his father an Oil Man – census. He marries Amy Elizabeth Gurr in 1893 in West Ham – Marriage Record. They have three children together, Winifred Amy Cutbush born 1895, Victoria Irene Cutbush born in 1897 and Gladys Cutbush born 1900 – Birth Record. Sadly, Lionel passes away in the same year his last child was born, 1900 – Death Record.
86 Later Censuses.
87 Death Record.
88 Marriage Record.
89 Born in 1856 in Highgate – Birth Record.
90 Born in 1858 in Highgate – Birth Record. He becomes an Insurance Clerk, passing away at only the age of twenty four in 1882 in Islington – Death Record.
91 Born 1860 in Highgate – Birth Record. She marries Charles Coldwell in 1888 in Islington – Marriage Record. They have three children together, Eric Holden Coldwell born in 1890 in Hornsey, Nesta Beatrice Coldwell in 1894 and Vera Isabel Coldwell born in 1894 in Hornsey – Birth Records.
92 Born in 1865 in Islington – Birth Record. He marries Margaret Elizabeth Boulton in 1893 in Edmonton – Marriage Record. They have three children together, Lilian Margaret Holden born 1894 in

Manor Park Cemetery. Where Reuben Cutbush, Charles Henry's Great Cousin is buried (above). ©Amanda Harvey Purse.

View of St Michael's church, where Reuben was baptised and married from Highgate Cemetery (right). ©Amanda Harvey Purse

---

Stroud Green, Violet Minerva Holden in 1896 in Edmonton and Pearle Minnie Holden in 1897 in Stroud Green – Birth Records.
93 Death Record.

Cutbush and Sons Family Business
– *Nurserymen Cont.*

This leaves James Cutbush, the second son to William and Sarah Cutbush and he was the one that carries on the family nursery business in Highgate, making it the success we now know it to be later on.

James married Elizabeth Mary Ann Hickman[94] in 1855 in Edmonton[95]. They had eleven children together, Elizabeth Annie Cutbush born in 1857, who passes away in 1881[96], Herbert James Cutbush born in 1858[97] (we will be mentioning Herbert in more detail later).

The next child was Edith Mary Cutbush, born in 1861[98], Alice Maud Cutbush born in 1863[99], Isabel Tracey Cutbush born in 1864[100], William Hickman Cutbush born in 1866[101], (we will also discuss William Hickman's family tree later on in the book)

Ernest George Cutbush born in 1868[102], Laura Jane Cutbush born in 1870[103], Ethel Louise Cutbush born in

---

94 Born on 12th August 1831 in Clerkenwell – Birth Record.
95 Marriage Record.
96 Birth and Death Record.
97 Birth Record.
98 Birth Record.
99 Birth Record.
100 Birth Record.
101 Birth Record.
102 Birth Record.
103 Birth Record.

1873[104], Amy Dalton Cutbush born in 1875[105] and *finally* Jessie Grace Cutbush born in 1878[106].

One may wonder how large the house had to be to hold this side of the Cutbush family at this time, with also having the servants such as Elizabeth Trimm, Harriet Starling, Lily Marie Jones and the nursemaid Martha Langmead all living within the house as well.[107]

However, a look for the children's name in the boarding school records shows as that Herbert was sent to Brunswick House in Barnet and William plus Ernest were sent to Totteridge Park in Hertford[108], so they were away from home.

This was something the family continued to do as when the head of the household passes away, as Amy can be seen on the records of the Royal Masonic Girls School[109] and Jessie was recorded as a boarder at London Orphans School in Watford[110] later on.

…

The Cutbush and Sons family nursery business was described in the local press by stating,

'A couple of centuries ago some enterprising and shrewd horticulturist had set up business as a nurseryman on the top of Highgate Hill, securing a position with a slight slope to the south

---

104 Birth Record.
105 Birth Record.
106 Birth Record.
107 1861 to 1881 censuses.
108 School Records.
109 In 1891.
110 School Records.

and upon this same spot there has, during the intervening years, been a continuation of a similar business. Still more remarkable is the fact that an ancestor of the present proprietors – a Cutbush – was carrying on the business of a nurseryman at the time when old William Curtis commenced to issue that wonderful work, the 'Botanical Magazine' from his botanic garden at Lambeth Marsh.'[111]

The article carries on by stating,

'The Messrs Cutbush have now four establishments. The central one in Highgate is devoted chiefly to the seed and bulb departments, plants under glass and ornamental trees and shrubs; at the North end enormous quantities of plants suitable for summer bedding and for window box gardening are cultivated but the demand is larger than supply'.[112]

A description was then made of the Barnet Branch in which it was stated that they had fruit trees, roses, hollies, ornamental trees and conifers to be sold to the public, while the Finchley branch had herbaceous plants, strawberries and bush fruits[113].

As we have seen in a family dispute stated previously, events were not always easy for James as owning a big, profitable business sometimes brought a few problems. In 1869, James was in the police courts due to an 'alleged embezzlement by a gardener at Highgate'.[114]

John Brown had been arrested by Inspector Westlake of Y Division, being charged with defrauding James, his employer by embezzling money from the Cutbush family business.

---

111 1st February 1901 – Barnet Press.
112 1st February 1901 – Barnet Press.
113 1st February 1901 – Barnet Press.
114 2nd June 1869 - Clerkenwell News and London Times.

John Brown had been working for James for six years and was the manager for any 'jobbing work'.

He had called upon Mrs. Fanny Herae of Hampstead Lane, a customer of James' and who owed him '12s 6d', to claim the money, this John Brown did not have the right to do.

She paid him and thought nothing more of it, until two weeks later, she received a bill to pay up from James Cutbush.

John Brown, at first denied he had visited her, but then admitted it. This was not the first time John Brown had done this, as it found out in court that he had actually embezzled about three hundred pounds from James, overall[115].

…

James had become a Freemason of the same lodge his older brother, William had joined, Gladsmuir Lodge number 1385 and 'served the office of W.M in 1876'[116].

He was also a member of the Gladsmuir Chapter, being a Steward for the Girl's School and Benevolent Institution and twice for the Boys' School. This led him to be a Life Governor for all the before said charities[117].

In 1875 and various *later* years, James was one of the judges at the International Fruit Show held at Alexandra Palace in Highgate.

---

[115] 2nd June 1869 - Clerkenwell News and London Times.
[116] 2nd June 1869 - Clerkenwell News and London Times.
[117] 8th August 1885 – Freemason.

The evening was often celebrated by a Venetian fete with a display of waterworks, fireworks and a procession of boats with coloured lights on the lake.

There were performances from the Jackley Troupe of Russian Athletes, Mr. F Maccabe, the Burgess Minstrels and a balloon ascent, performed in one year by one Mr. Edmund Reid[118].

At the time, Edmund Reid had completed this ascent, he was a newly made policeman that was currently working in the area of London called the Elephant and Castle[119].

However, he would later also be involved in the investigation of the Jack the Ripper case in 1888, writing a certain report that our *Charles Henry Cutbush* would also have seen[120].

By 1882, James had also become the treasurer of the Highgate Horticultural Society, with the annual meetings being held at the Literary and Scientific Institution. Sadly, just three years later James passes away.

James was attending a fruit and flower show, where he and Baroness Burdett-Courtts were handing out prizes. When the crowds were cheering and thanking James for adding some of his own flowers for decoration for the event, James took to the stage and before he could say a word back, he

---

118 11th September 1875 – Hampstead and Highgate Express.
[119] Please see Inspector Reid: The Real Ripper Street by Amanda Harvey Purse for more information on Edmund Reid.
120 Please see Inspector Reid: The Real Ripper Street by Amanda Harvey Purse for more information on Edmund Reid.

was gripped by an apoplectic fit and fell forwards towards the crowd.[121]

The doctor was called and while James had slightly recovered, he was taken home, where sadly he was seized with another fit and died at midnight on the Saturday 1st August 1885.

His fifty eighth birthday.

---

121 8th August 1885 – The Barnet Press.

Author at Highgate Cemetery.

The gates at Highgate Cemetery, the coffins of the Cutbush family would have been taken through this, heading towards us. ©Amanda Harvey Purse.

...

The funeral took place on 6th August 1885 at the very nearby Highgate Cemetery. The coffin in which James laid in, was first taken into the church where the service was read by Reverend T. Trinder with Reverend Mackenzie playing the organ for the people entering and once again when they left the church.

The coffin was then followed to the grave side by a large crowd of mourners, where the service continued and flowers of the best quality were laid by the family and friends, while the Freemasons of the crowd threw twigs of Acacia into the grave[122].

Newspapers recorded the event and by stating,

'Like poor old Joe Clarke or Tom Pinch, as he was frequently called from his likeness to one of Dickens' favourite characters, Mr James Cutbush formed one of the corner stones of local life at Highgate their removal one after another will leave a blank that none but the most energetic and kind-hearted can ever hope to make good...The funeral procession also included a number of the deceased's workmen and several of the chief horticulturists around the metropolis, besides many residents in Highgate and the deepest sympathy is universally expressed with the family in their bereavement.'[123]

This description can show us how well-liked James Cutbush was to not only the community in which he lived, worked and helped in but how his death was seen as an *empty gap* laid in the town.

---

[122] 8th August 1885 – The Barnet Press.
[123] 8th August 1885 – The Barnet Press.

Also, the newspaper's description of him is wonderfully quirky. In a book where we are trying to see through all the details and facts belonging to a person to picture the actual human being underneath, this description is a perfect one as if gives us not just a physical description of him but it also highlights his personality to us researchers today.

It is also interesting to note that at this time, Charles Henry, was also well known in his own role in London, being a policeman and he would have been old enough to have known of this death.

So, with that being stated, could we then wonder if he was there at the funeral and if he knew how the area thought of his family?

...

This leaves James' children to carry on the family tree, so let us mention any information we have on the females within the family first.

With Elizabeth Annie Cutbush, she sadly had passed away four years before her own father at the age of twenty four[124]. Edith Mary Cutbush meanwhile had married Francis Richard Barrell, two years after the death of her father[125].

They move away from the capital and lived in Bristol where they go on to have two children together there, Francis Maxwell Barrell on the 16th March 1892 and Kenneth Cecil Barrell born on 14th April 1896, who passes

---

[124] In 1881 – Death Record.
[125] Marriage Record.

away at the ripe age of eighty eight years in 1984, in Uckfield, Sussex[126].

Isabel Tracey Cutbush married Samuel Huggins in 1889[127] and they have one child, which they name Barbara Huggins in 1900[128] and with Laura Jane Cutbush, she sadly died at the age of eight in 1878[129].

---

[126] Birth and Death Records.
[127] Marriage Record.
[128] Birth Record.
[129] Death Record.

Cutbush and Sons Family Business
– Another generation takes on the nursery

The males of James's children start with Herbert James Cutbush. He was an interesting man and a sign that he was well known could be highlighted in the fact that he is listed amongst the 'who's who' that are buried in Highgate Cemetery on its website, but let us start from the beginning.

Born in 1858 to James and Elizabeth Mary Ann Cutbush, in 1861, Herbert was living at Gothia Cottage in St Pancras with his parents[130].

Ten years later, Herbert was sent to Wood Street Brunswick House (a boarding school) in Barnet[131]. At the age of twenty two, Herbert was back living back with his parents at Number 1 West Hill, Highgate, where he was working with his father as a nurseryman.[132]

He married Grace Emma Maile (born 1859 in St Pancras[133]) one year later in 1882 in St Pancras[134].

On 20th January 1883, Herbert and Grace have their first child, which Herbert uses his own name with his son's middle name as they called him William Herbert Leonard Cutbush and the family were living on the premises of the nursery in West Hill[135].

---

[130] 1861 Census.
[131] 1871 Census.
[132] 1881 Census.
[133] Birth Record.
[134] Marriage Record.
[135] 1891 Census. They were living there with servant, Adeline Poor.

Although the first child was recorded as being born William Herbert Leonard Cutbush, sometimes he was known as just 'Herbert' and in the later censuses his name changes to just 'Leonard Cutbush'[136].

Two years later, with the death of his father, Herbert takes on the now well-known nursery business. Herbert himself adds to the family business by first receiving a silver gilt medal from The National Chrysanthemum Society.

This led the Cutbush's to gain the contract for planting bulbs and flowers at Highgate Cemetery, where he and most of Herbert's family members lay today[137].

In the spirit of trying to get to know the personalities within the Cutbush family, we find an interesting article about Herbert.

Instead of mentioning him in the world of gardening, in the Hampstead and Highgate Express of 1887, we see him playing cricket for Mr. H. Burrows' Eleven against Mr. W. Davis' Eleven. Herbert, played a 'capital' innings of fifty eight[138].
Similarly, it is interesting to note that Herbert's wife, Grace had a hobby and amazingly, through research, we today, can know what that was.

She was a singer. Being recorded as 'Mrs H. Cutbush', she was a part of the evening entertainment held at the Vestry Hall in Hampstead on the 13th January 1887.

---

136 1901 Census.
137 7th November 1896 – Hampstead and Highgate Express.
138 13Th September 1887 – Hampstead and Highgate Express.

Prices were ranging from five shillings to two shillings and of course the floral decorations were completed by a family business called William Cutbush and Son, Highgate, *which we may know of now*[139].

...

In 1893, Herbert becomes a Freemason of the Hortus Lodge Number 2469[140], he pays his membership fee until 1909.

A year after him becoming a Freemason, in early September of 1894, Herbert shows us not just the kindness of him but the uniqueness of him being an employer. So unique in fact that this event was recorded in the local paper, stating,

'On Saturday nearly a hundred of the employees of Messrs W. Cutbush and Son of the Highgate, Finchley and Barnet Nurseries, the firm which supplied the whole of the bulbs used this spring in the parks and open spaces under the control of London County Council and in Royal Parks, including Hyde Park and also the whole of the shrubs planted in the new park at Dulwich, went to Margate for their annual holiday.'[141]

The workers had to pay into a fund to help the cost of the holiday, however when the day came, Herbert surprised his workers by giving them back their money and paying for the whole holiday, himself.

They travelled from Barnet and Highgate by an early boat train express, which had two carriages reserved for them, to

---

139 8th January 1887 – Hampstead and Highgate Express.
140 Freemason Records.
141 8th September 1894 – Barnet Press.

Chatham, where they changed to carry on their journey to Margate, getting there by half past ten in the morning.

As soon as they departed from the train, most of the men headed towards Margate Pier to watch La Marguerite (a boat) come in to the pier and then head of again for France.

Afterwards, they went to the Queen's Arms Hotel, where dinner was served to them. Herbert sat at the head of the table with his brother, William Hickman Cutbush.

The crowd of workers applauded their employer, for his good reputation, in which Herbert thanked everyone, saying he was so glad to see many of his employees enjoying themselves but felt guilty that there were a few that had to stay behind, but asked to have a drink in their healths.

William Hickman Cutbush, Herbert's brother had just got married, so toasts were made in his and his wife's honour, but by half seven pm they all started their travels back to London, reaching the capital just two hours later[142].

It could be suggested that this occasion shows us a lot about Herbert, how he was novel enough to take his employees on holiday and go with them, within this time period.

It can also show that he seemed to allow his workmen into his own personal life and share the happy times with them.

...

---

142 8th September 1894 – Barnet Press.

On the 1901 census, Herbert and his family were recorded at living at Number 47 West Hill with servant, Lois Tabbitt, who was aged just twenty three[143].

Herbert and Grace were forty three years old by this census and their son was recorded, as mentioned before, as Leonard Cutbush.

In 1904, Herbert appears in a book called The Book of Topiary by Charles Henry Curtis, in it, it states,

'In the revival of Topiary in England no single person has taken a deeper interest that Mr. Herbert J. Cutbush... Mr. H. J. Cutbush has frequently visited Holland and he has travelled through and through the little country until he knows it, horticulturally, far better than even many eminent Dutch nurseryman do.' [144]

When the revival of Topiary first happened, Herbert travelled to Holland almost every weekend to learn what the Dutch nursery trade was doing, he took samples of their work to see if he would use them in the local churchyard and cemetery back home[145].

What an interesting view we have here of an Cutbush, searching for the latest trends, even if that means to travel away from England, a sign perhaps of a Cutbush willing to do anything all in the aim to make his job better.

Perhaps these are traits we see later in Charles Henry Cutbush as he progresses in his career as a policeman?

---

143 1901 Census.
144 The Book of Topiary 1904 – Charles Henry Curtis and William Gibson.
145 The Book of Topiary 1904 – Charles Henry Curtis and William Gibson.

...

In 1906, Herbert was still playing his cricket. Playing for Crouch End when they were against Friern Barnet in the July of that year[146].

On 23rd February 1910, Herbert gets called to Marylebone Police court under the Prevention of Corruption Act of 1906.

He had been accused of 'knowingly' giving John Brown, a gardener that worked for another company owned by Earl Cowley, an account of goods supplied that totalled the sum of '£279 1s 9d' which were false.

He was also accused of 'corruptly' giving and taking a gallon of whisky to Charles Kidd, another gardener who worked in Lancaster.[147]

However, after Herbert spoke in court stating 'there was no concealment about the gift of whisky to Kidd'[148] and that it was only a Christmas present, something he always sent out 'to old customers and old friends'.[149]

Also with Herbert telling the court 'very frankly' that he had been sending out Christmas presents for the last twenty five years, he was then found to be not guilty of any charges, two months later.[150]

It is interesting to note that the Judge stated,

---

[146] 11th July 1906 – Islington Gazette.
[147] Bognor Regis Observer - 2nd March 1910.
[148] Northern Daily Telegraph - 18th April 1910.
[149] Northern Daily Telegraph - 18th April 1910.
[150] Ross Gazette - 21st April 1910

'This was very important case, and as far as he knew it was the first under the Act, though he might be wrong. The character of well known people was at stake in the case, and when he heard the nature of the more serious charge made against people whom he knew occupied a high position in the horticultural world he was startled to hear the suggestion made that Messrs Cutbush could have been guilty of one of the most serious crimes known to the law.'[151]

Ten years later, the family were living at Norman Hurst, Broadlands Road in North Highgate. Herbert and his wife were in their early fifties and their son Leonard, at the age of twenty eight, was following in his father's footsteps by being a nurseryman.

The family also have two servants, both sisters, Annie and Florence Fisk[152]. On the 1911 census, Herbert's home had listed that he had twelve rooms including the kitchen[153].

Sadly, seven years later, on 7th March 1918[154], Herbert passes away at the age of fifty nine, being buried in Highgate Cemetery. His passing doesn't go unnoticed even today, as he is one of the many names mention on the Highgate Cemetery website.

When we consider the size of the cemetery and the amount of people that lay there, it is wonderful to see Herbert's name still being mentioned, after all this time.

...

---

[151] Northern Daily Telegraph - 18th April 1910.
[152] 1911 Census.
[153] 1911 Census.
[154] Death Record.

Considering so many of this side of the Cutbush family were buried within the, some say, haunted grounds of Highgate Cemetery, the author felt it was only right to visit the place to pay her last respects.

The author would like to point out that, she never came across a ghost while she spent a few hours there. However, she did find it somewhat strange that, when she finally did manage to find the Cutbush's graves, through all the long grass, nettles, trees and other headstones of which the cemetery has plenty, there was, almost as a marker to draw in this *animal loving author*, a large, well maintained but possibly feral tabby cat sitting on the actual headstone the author wanted to find. *You can make of that what you will.*

The author started her search by contacting and eventually meeting with Highgate Cemetery staff, who were very welcoming and kind enough to allow the author to visit the Cutbush's last resting places that was off the beaten track.

So, with a few hand drawn maps and a walkie talkie, for Health and Safety reasons in tow, she began to make her search for the graves.

Up the stone steps that are worn with time to a winding pathway, with beautiful trees and historical headstones all facing the path as if they were there to greet anyone that passes by.

A slight turn to the right and then to the left, under the Egyptian arch, which was once an entrance to a pyramid to hold coffins like a catacomb. However, families thought the place to be too dark to house their loved ones and eventually the 'roof' of the pyramid was taken off, leaving just the arch today[155].

As you walk under the archway, by natural impulse your eyes gaze upwards, they pass the door in front of you, beyond to the large tree that looks as if it sits on the roof of the building and further on to a tall, grey spire that belongs to St Michael's Church.

Turn to the right and head towards a set of stairs and the headstones in front of you are where the known people of the commerce trade lay. Herbert's last resting place is situated slightly to the left of the stairway and a few rows back.

His grave has beautifully surrounded itself by the nature of Highgate. The headstone is of a stony Celtic cross that seems to suit the area it sits in.

Herbert's name appears at the bottom, still visible after all these years, but he is not alone for his wife's name is mentioned underneath and to the left-hand side of the cross is his son's name, his full name being recorded of William Herbert Leonard Cutbush.

Father, mother and son all together in a patch of greenery surrounded by trees and the wild flowers in the ever-growing capital that they all would have known. In addition, because of their backgrounds working in nurseries all their lives, this just seemed to be an area that was very apt for the family.

---

[155] Highgate Cemetery Tour information.

The author also fully admits that she tapped the stone cross three times and quietly said a few respectful words to them, hoping that they like her work, of what she is trying to do in this book and can see she really does care for them, even without ever meeting them, before she left the way she came.

...

At the time of Herbert's passing, he was still living at Number 19 Broadland – Road, Highgate, he left '£5808 8s 2d' to be shared between Sydney Herbert Maile, his brother in law and to William Edward Holland, his accountant[156]. Which is a little strange as his wife was still alive and so was his son, however they do not get mentioned in his probate, *but are buried with him.*

After the death of her husband, Grace left London and two years later she passes away in Aberystwyth, Wales at the age of sixty one[157]. Although she may have died in Wales, she was buried with her husband in Highgate Cemetery, London.

Their son, 'Leonard' had married Flora Hilda Vardon on the 30th July 1913[158], in the church of St Brelade, Jersey, passing away himself in Bon Air Nursing Home, Jersey on 11th May 1959. However, again as already mentioned, he was not buried there, being buried in Highgate Cemetery, London[159].

...

---

156 Herbert's Probate.
157 In 1920 – Death Record.
158 Marriage Record.
159 Death Record.

Author at the Cutbush's Family plot at Highgate Cemetery.

The Cutbush's Family plot at Highgate Cemetery. ©Amanda Harvey Purse.

Herbert's name on his headstone. ©Amanda Harvey Purse

We have already mentioned that Herbert was working with his brother William Hickman Cutbush to run the nurseries. William was running the Barnet department, as in the 1891 census we can see that he was living there, like his relation before him[160].

Three years later, William married Jessie Stevens in Barnet and in 1896[161], the couple had their first child, Douglas Cutbush[162] (we will mention Douglas in more detail later).

In 1902, the couple had their second son on 17th March, considering the date, we can imagine, why the couple named him *Patrick* Cutbush[163].

On the 1911 census, the family were still living in Barnet, all a part from Patrick Cutbush, who at the age of nine years old was living with his aunt in Chipping, Barnet[164].

When William's brother, Herbert passes away in 1918, William takes on the whole family business on his own and two years later William and his wife Jessie move to New Road Gardens in Enfield[165]. Sadly, just one year later William has to cope with a death of his mother, Elizabeth Mary Ann Hickman Cutbush on the 7th January 1921[166].

The author has had the chance to see William Hickman Cutbush's handwriting within an item that is now in the author's collection.

---

160 1891 Census.
161 Marriage Record.
162 Birth Record.
163 17th March is St Patrick's Day.
164 1911 Census.
165 Electoral Register.
166 Death Record.

It is a business invoice, numbered 970, for a customer of the William Cutbush and Son, Nurserymen, Seedsmen and Florist[167] family business. A customer named Colonel Lovell of Millfield Lane, Highgate.

It was dated the 31st March 1922 and it covered three days' work, the first being 27th February 1922, the 28th and 3rd March 1922, in which the Colonel paid for three men, fifty turf pieces and other items such as 'one ball of twine' for five pounds, fourteen shillings and three pence.[168]

To actually see the handwriting of someone we are researching is a marvellous thing, as it literally is bringing history alive, before our very eyes.

...

By 1936, William and Jessie move further out of London to be living at Gillian Cottage, Lowfield Heath, in Surrey[169].

Sadly, William's wife, Jessie, passed away in 1943 in St Albans and just six years later, William, himself, passes away on 6th November 1949[170].

---

[167] The heading description on the invoice. The invoice also states the business telephone numbers of 'No2 Barnet and 760 Hornsey' and that the business used 'Barclay and Co Bank' for their cheques and postal orders.
[168] William Cutbush and Son business invoice in the author's collection.
[169] Electoral Register.
[170] Death Records.

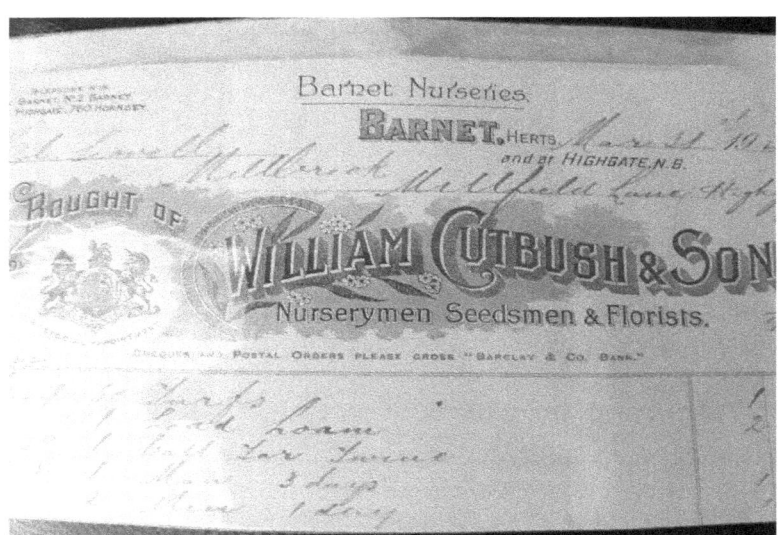

Invoice of the William Cutbush and Sons family, from the author's own collection (above). ©Amanda Harvey Purse.

William Cutbush's last resting place at Highgate Cemetery (right). ©Amanda Harvey Purse.

In his probate it states that William's last known address was Number 31 King Edward Road, East Barnet and that he left the sum of three hundred and sixty seven pounds, five shillings and four pence to his son Patrick who was an architect at the time.[171]

...

In 1927 William's son, Patrick marries Iva Francis Symmons in Barnet[172], a year later on the 2nd April 1928 Patrick and his wife travel to the Port of Southampton and board a ship to the United States of America.

This was one of their many trips to New York, another one being on 30th August 1936[173] and in that same year they also travel to Canada[174].

Patrick passes away at the age of sixty five in 1967 in Barnet[175].

This death is not just an ending of a life but also the end of the Cutbush family actually owning the nurseries in London. A business that had started in the 1820's, that we have just seen, had many highs and lows within its time.

A business that had grown to be a part of Highgate Cemetery and the Royal Parks of London but also a business that was known to the community.

With the death of Patrick, the Cutbush family then sold the nursery to the Highgate Cemetery themselves.[176]

---

171 Probate Records.
172 Marriage Record.
173 Travel lists.
174 20th September 1936 – Travel lists.
175 Death Record.

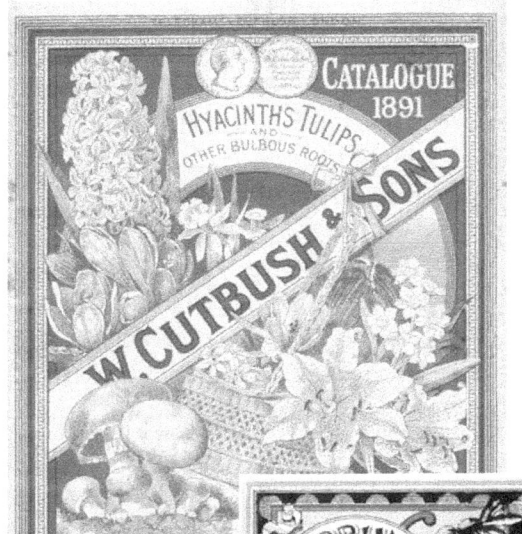

Two business signs showing the Cutbush family nursery business from the author's collection.

176 Highgate Cemetery history told by the kind staff to the author.

A Cutbush Soldier
– through and through.

William Hickman Cutbush's older son Douglas Cutbush was baptised on the 5th April 1896 in Barnet[177]. By the age of five years old, he was living with his parents at the nursery in South Mimms, Barnet and when he reached school age, he, like his older brother, Patrick, went Judde House School[178].

Douglas left school in 1912, where he had picked up a keen interest in photography. After leaving school he had travelled to Holland's bulb farms and we can imagine he was with his father at this time. He also travelled elsewhere and saw nurseries in France.

We can wonder if his father, William, was hoping that Douglas would take over the family business after these trips, but if he did think this, the country going to war, changed the plans[179].

Douglas, was eager to join the army, however, the first time he signs up, he was turned away because of being 'medically unfit'.

He then turned to the Red Cross, but they didn't reply back to him, so because he was able to speak French, Flemish and Dutch, due to the experience he had picked up in the nurseries, *possibly with his father*, he volunteered to work with the Belgian refugees at Alexandra Palace in 1914, until he fell unwell in the Christmas season of that year[180].

---

[177] Birth and Baptism Record.
[178] School Records.
[179] Tonbridge School Records.
[180] Army Records - IWM

Another sign of his dedication to the army was that as soon as he was well, he applied again and this time he was allowed into 53rd Special Reserve of the Duke of Cambridge's Own Middlesex Regiment on the 7th June 1915.

In the October 1915 he was attached to a Regular Battalion when he went to the front line, he was wounded by a gunshot in his thigh on the 20th January 1916 because of which, he had to spend nine weeks in a French hospital[181].

When he returned, he was given light duties within his own regiment, however this did not last long, as by the 10th November 1916 he had been promoted to Lewis Machine Gun Officer and was a part of the advancement on Beaumont Hamel.

Douglas was ordered to go and find Two Companies to help to advance to the front line and to take charge of the situation. He held his position under very heavy fire until the order came to retire, for these actions he was given the Military Cross[182].

In the February of 1917 he was promoted to Acting Captain and he had command of 'A' Company, sadly on the 10th April 1917, Douglas passed away from being shot in the head while under heavy machine gun and sniper fire near Monchy, France.[183] He was only twenty one years old.

His father, William, was sent Douglas's portrait, with the words,

---

181 Army Records - IWM
182 Army Records - IWM
183 Army Records - IWM

'With deep regret I have to announce to you the death of your son. The loss is our loss as well as yours, as he was exceptionally keen, brave and capable officer and greatly beloved by all his brother officers. He led his company, of which he had command, with skill and judgment and exposed his own person with an absolute disregard of danger', written by in Commanding Officer[184].

Douglas was buried at Level Crossing Cemetery in Plot l. A. 9, at Fampoux, Pas De Calais in France, on his headstone are the words,

'He sought the glory of his country and found the glory of God'[185]

This is where we leave this side of Cutbush family, which originally stemmed from *Charles Henry's Great Uncle, William Cutbush.*

We now turn to William's brother, Charles *Henry's Grandfather, James Cutbush.*

---

[184] Army Records - IWM
[185] Information from Level Crossing Cemetery.

A Man of Many Children

James Cutbush was born on the 9th December 1781 to John and Ann Cutbush in the Kent village of Sandhurst[186] and he was baptised in the church of St Nicholas, almost a month later on the 6th January 1782[187].

At the age of twenty four, on the Christmas Eve of 1805, James was entering into St Alphege Church in Greenwich to marry Lucy Jeater[188], who was three years older than him and came from Abinger in Surrey[189].

Two years later they have their first born, Eliza Cutbush, on 19th November 1806[190], the fact that she was born and baptised in Lewisham, does suggested the family were still living near London at this point[191] however, by the birth of their second child in 1808, they had returned to Kent.

Eliza Cutbush, Charles Henry's Aunt, marries on 3rd April 1828[192] to John Epps[193] and have one child, who they name Eliza Louisa Epps[194]. By 1841, the Epps family were living

---

186 Birth Record.
187 Baptism Record.
188 Marriage Record.
189 Birth Record.
190 Birth Record.
191 Baptised on the 14th December 1806 in St Mary's Church, Lewisham – Baptism Record.
192 Marriage Record.
193 Born in1804 in Boughton Aluph – Birth Record. Baptised on the 30th September 1804 – Baptism Record.
194 Born in 1830 in Willesborough, Kent – Birth Record. Baptised on 28th February 1830 – Baptism Record. She went on to marry George William Cummins (Born 1828 – 1887: Birth and Death Record) on 17th July 1852 in the church of St James, Dover in Kent – Marriage Record.

in John's birth town of Boughton Aluph[195] near Ashford and by the next census we discover that John was working as a gardener[196].

By 1871, the couple were living with their daughter and her husband at Number 47 Somerset Road, Ashford, with the daughter's husband being listed as a Railway Clerk/mechanic[197].

…

This was an important job to have in the town of Ashford at the time. The reason for this was because, although Ashford has often been described as a market town, (a description that has sadly been lost over the years, due to the 'market' moving to the outskirts of the town and the area it once was is now the *second* cinema for the town) it has also been described as a Railway town.

The local library still has a whole section dedicated to the railway in its museum part and the town's railway station was even mentioned in a Sherlock Holmes adventure, The Final Problem[198] as well as other stories[199].

We will also see how Somerset Road in the main area of Ashford town was quite a popular area for relations of the Cutbush family later on.

---

[195] 1841 Census.
[196] 1851 Census.
[197] 1871 Census.
[198] Written by Sir Arthur Conan Doyle.
[199] The Strange Case of Caroline Maxwell by Amanda Harvey Purse, *for example*.

Some of the houses in which the family would have seen, in Somerset Road still exists today and are situated on the ring road of the main town.

The Victorian houses mainly consisted of an attic room in the eves of the house, connected to, quite often, a winding stairway, down to two large bedrooms and one room that could have been used for a servant or a bathroom if there wasn't one outside.

Go down one more level and we would have been faced with what we would call, the living room, which could be transferred into the sick room for any household member.

A small kitchen would be at the back of the house, with a set of stairs leading down to the cellar, where coal deliveries would have been made[200].

By 1881, the family had moved again but not far to Willesborough Lees[201], once again the mother, daughter and husband are all living together.

However, the father, John, was not listed as he had passed away on the 11th June 1878[202]. Eliza, the mother, passes away three years after the census, on the 15th November 1884[203]. The daughter's husband, George passes away on the 9th January 1887 with his wife *Eliza, Charles Henry's Cousin,* passing away on 29th April 1896[204]. The same year that Charles Henry, himself, passes away.

---

200 An author visits to 33 Somerset Road.
201 1881 Census.
202 Death Record.
203 Death Record.
204 Death Records.

Author at a Victorian house along Somerset Road, Ashford.

Author with a Victorian dress found in the attic of a house in Somerset Road.

Considering that a member of the Cutbush family that lived in Somerset Road, where the attics connect to each other, was a dressmaker, this item might be an important find.

...

James and Lucy Cutbush's next child was born in 1808 in the area of Willesborough, near Ashford in Kent, they name him Henry Cutbush and baptised him on the 11th December 1808[205].

Henry sadly passes away, five years later, on the 17th December 1813, being buried on the 19th December 1813 in Willesborough[206].

James and Lucy's third child were born in 1810, in Willesborough, they name him Frederick Cutbush and baptised him on 11th November 1810[207].

Frederick, Charles Henry's uncle, moves to the capital and marries on 23rd October 1832 in All Hallows the Great church, in the City of London[208] to Ann East[209].

Their first child was born in 1833 in the City of London, they name her Ann Cutbush, however sadly the child passes away just two years later on 8th June 1835 in Stratford in Bow, London[210].

Their next child, Thomas Frederick Cutbush[211], was born just two months after the death of their first child, on 13th

---

205 Birth and Baptism Record.
206 Death and Burial Records.
207 Birth and Baptism Record.
208 Marriage Record.
209 Born on 16th September 1811 in Middlesex – Birth Record. Baptised on 6th October 1811 – Baptism Record.
210 Birth and Death Record.
211 By 1851, Thomas was living with his uncle James Minton in The Stag Public House, London – 1851 Census. He then has two children, another Thomas Frederick Cutbush (1858 – 1941) – Birth

August 1835, being baptised in the same church Frederick and Ann had married in[212]. Thomas Frederick passes away on the 1st May 1918, being buried on the 9th May 1918 in Southwark, London[213].

Frederick and Ann Cutbush have their next child, James Cutbush, on the 1st August in the 1830's in Upper Thames Street, City of London, who sadly passes away on the 8th January 1838 at Number 84 Upper Thames Street[214].

Their next child, who they name Charles Cutbush was born on 3rd January 1839, in the City of London, being baptised in All Hallows the Great Church on the 2nd February that year[215].

---

and Death Record and Alice Fry Cutbush (1860 – 1937) – Birth and Death Record. By 1861 Thomas was living with his children at Number 5 Chester Street Lambeth – 1861 Census and by the next year, he has another child, who he names Charles Cutbush (1862 – 1937) – Birth and Death Record. On the 1871 census, he was still living with his 'wife' Marian and children in Lambeth, being a clerk, this role changed ten years later to Commercial Traveller when they were living at Number 104 Faraday Street – 1881 Census. Six years later Thomas officially marries Marian Fry, on the 6th June 1887 in the church of St John the Evangelist in Lambeth – Marriage Record.

212 Birth and Baptism Record.
213 Death and Burial Record.
214 Birth and Death Record.
215 Birth and Baptism Record. This Charles Cutbush marries Mary Frances Foster on 2nd February 1860 in Presbyterian Church in Victoria, Australia and has a number of children there – Marriage Record. Ellen Foster Cutbush (1860 – 1934) – Birth and Death Records, Frederick Cutbush born in 1862 – Birth Record, Lucy Ann Cutbush born 1864 – Birth Record and Catherine Cutbush born 1866 -Birth Record. Charles then moves to New Zealand and has Mary Ann Cutbush born 1869 and who passes away a year later, on 11th November 1870 – Birth and Death Record and Mary Frances Cutbush born 1872, who passes away in 1873 in the West Coast of New Zealand – Birth and Death Record.

The next child Frederick and Ann have was Eliza Cutbush[216], born in 1840 and baptised on the 8th November 1840 in Kennington, Kent[217], this baptism show us that Frederick had moved back to Kent by this time period.

Eliza was not the only child they had in 1840, Eliza would seem to have been a twin, as Frederick and Ann have another child, they name her Rebecca Cutbush, however she sadly passes away, a year later in 1841[218].

By 1842, Frederick and Ann had another child, they name him Joseph Jepson Cutbush[219]. On the 23rd May 1878 this Joseph married Maria Logsdon in Baldock, Hertfordshire and by 1881 the couple were living in West Ham, London[220]. Joseph passes away on the 11th March 1895 in Peckham[221].

In 1843, Frederick files for bankruptcy[222], something that was no doubt hard on the family that was ever growing as

---

216 Eliza married Thomas Worger Piddlesden (1841 – 1917) – Birth and Death Record, in 1864 – Marriage Record. In 1876, they have their only child, Clara Piddlesden – Birth Record. By 1881 the couple were living at Number 19 Queens Street Ashford, a road not that far away from Somerset Road, mentioned earlier. Thomas being listed as a Brass Moulder – 1881 Census. By 1911, the Piddlesden family were living a few roads along from Queens Street, to Number 3 Barrow Hill – 1911 Census. Eliza passes away on 8th March 1912 and was buried on 14th March 1912 within the main church in the town of Ashford, St Mary's – Death and Burial Records.
217 Birth and Baptism Record.
218 Birth and Death Record.
219 Birth Record.
220 1881 Census.
221 Death Record.
222 Bradford Observer - 9th February 1843.

Frederick and Ann have another five children after this point.

That being, Ellen Cutbush (1844 – 1872[223]), Lucy Ann Cutbush (1845 – 1865[224]), Robert Henry Cutbush born 1847, Jane Cutbush (1848 – 1849[225]) and finally Walter Cutbush who was born in 1850 but sadly only lived for thirteen days[226].

With Frederick being Charles Henry's uncle, all of his vast number of children would have been Charles Henry's cousins, some of which had spent time in London.

With this known one wonders if Charles Henry knew of them?

...

Frederick's parents, James and Lucy have more aunts and uncles of Charles Henry, the next one being Caroline Cutbush, baptised on 2nd May 1813 in Willesborough, Kent[227].

She married Robert Franklyn Redhouse (1813 – 1865)[228] on the 6th November 1837 in Hastings[229], although Robert was a tailor living in Gloucester Place, Old Kent Road by the time of his marriage, three years later he was claiming

---

[223] Birth and Death Records.
[224] Birth and Death Records.
[225] Birth and Death Records.
[226] Birth and Death Records.
[227] Baptism Record.
[228] Birth and Death Records.
[229] Marriage Record.

bankruptcy[230] and having to move to a place his new wife probably knew better that himself.

By 1851 they were living in New Street, Ashford[231], Robert was still a tailor. New Street was and is still very close to Somerset Road, an address we have mentioned before for the Cutbush family.

In 1863, two years before Caroline's husband, Robert, passes away we see that Robert owns a premise in Hotel Street, on the corner of Friar Lane in Leicester and that he had turned his attention to a Midland 'Haircutting, shampooing and Toilet Article Establishment', where his Hydraulic Shampooing Apparatus was working in good order with hot and cold water[232].

After the death of her husband in 1865 and by 1871 Caroline were actually living within Somerset Road, at Number 16.

Although Caroline's husband had passed away, she carries on his business by being a dressmaker, herself[233]. Caroline passes away on the 25th January 1888 and was buried on the 1st February 1888 in St Mary's Church, the main church in Ashford town[234].

It is interesting to note that the author found a Victorian handmade dress in the attic of the house she visited in Somerset Road.

---

230 Birmingham Journal - 7th November 1840.
231 1851 Census,
232 Leicester Journal - 11th December 1863.
233 1871 Census.
234 Death and Burial Records.

Considering that the attic runs through a number of homes on that row, could it be possible that the dress she found was made by Caroline Redhouse, Charles Henry Cutbush's aunt?

The next child James and Lucy have was William Cutbush, and it is from his branch of the Cutbush family tree that Charles Henry mainly has connections to Cutbush's in Australia.

The Australian Connection

This *William Cutbush was Charles Henry's uncle,* born in 1815 in Willesborough, he was baptised on the 2nd April 1815 in the Parish Church in Willesborough[235].

He marries Elizabeth Back[236] on the 22nd June 1836[237], their marriage was even recorded in the local newspaper at the time.[238]

The first child the couple have, they name William Henry Cutbush, baptising him on 9th August 1837 in the main church of Ashford town, St Mary's[239]. *Where Charles Henry himself, would be baptised, only seven years later.*

He becomes a commercial traveller but sadly, William, passes away at the age of twenty four, on the 17th December 1861 in Hythe[240] and he left one hundred pounds to his father, William[241].

The next child William and Elizabeth had was George Back Cutbush, born on the 30th April 1839, in the town of Ashford, being baptised on the 31st May 1840 in Hawkhurst[242].

---

[235] Birth and Baptism Records.
[236] Baptism was held on the 14th January 1813 in Westwell, passing away in1897 Elham – Baptism and Death Record.
[237] Marriage Record.
[238] South Eastern Gazette - 5th July 1836.
[239] Baptism Record.
[240] Death Record.
[241] William Henry Cutbush's probate.
[242] Birth and Baptism Record.

George Back Cutbush, Charles Henry's cousin, joins the navy as an Able Seaman in 1861, he then travelled on the ship called Ganges and arrived in Sydney, Australia on the 28th November 1863[243], he was to never return to England to live again.

He married Annie Murphy (1848 – 1919)[244] on the 23rd September 1866[245] and the couple have a number of children.

That being, Elizabeth Cutbush (1868 – 1952)[246], Annie Mary Magdalene Cutbush (1871 – 1946)[247], Georgina Mary Cutbush (1874 – 1945)[248], William Cutbush (1876 – 1878)[249], Florence Margaret Cutbush (1879 – 1929)[250], George Back Junior (1880 – 1881)[251], John Chillian Cutbush (1881 – 1912)[252], Joseph James Cutbush (1883 – 1884)[253], Elleen Malachy Cutbush, born in 1885[254], Estelle Josephine Cutbush (1888 – 1961)[255] and *finally* Thomas á Beckett Cutbush (1890 – 1972)[256].

All these children that were born in Australia would have been Charles Henry's first cousins once removed.

---

[243] Travel Records.
[244] Birth and Death Records.
[245] Marriage Record.
[246] Birth and Death Record.
[247] Birth and Death Record.
[248] Birth and Death Record.
[249] Birth and Death Record.
[250] Birth and Death Record.
[251] Birth and Death Record.
[252] Birth and Death Record.
[253] Birth and Death Record.
[254] Birth Record.
[255] Birth and Death Record.
[256] Birth and Death Record.

By 1891 George Back Cutbush and his wife Annie were living at Burwood, New South Wales in Australia. Five years later, George being registered as living at the Treasury Hotel in Queensland in the City directories of 1896[257]. The year of Charles Henry 's passing.

By 1905 George was living in Brisbane[258], North Queensland but sadly on the Christmas Day of 1913, George passes away, being buried on the 31st December 1913 in Nudgee Catholic Cemetery, in Brisbane Australia[259].

It is slightly interesting that Charles Henry's cousin was a Roman Catholic. This is because when we can consider what Charles Henry had been suggested as feeling about that certain religion, a few months prior to his death, which will be mention later in this book.

…

George Back Cutbush was not the only child of William and Elizabeth's to go to Australia, Charles Cutbush, born on 4th March 1842 in Tonbridge[260], Kent, later moved there after being a Grocer at Number 24 St Margaret's Street in Canterbury[261].

In an odd piece of local history, Number 24 St Margaret's Street, in Canterbury is today a fashionable clothing store. However, perhaps because of how long that building had

---

[257] 1891 Census and 1896 City Directories.
[258] City Directories.
[259] Death and Burial Records.
[260] Birth Record.
[261] 1861 Census.

been situated there and possibly because it is actually along a street that has been known to be the most haunted in Canterbury, the store has a few ghostly happenings attached it.

There are a number of stories about the customers and staff feeling and sometimes seeing a haunting spirit within the building, sometimes standing right behind them. There is also a story that a female skeleton is standing upright within one the pillars outside the shop[262].

Also, linking this building back to the Cutbush family, we can see that with Charles Henry's cousin, Charles, working as a Grocer at this address, he would have been just an eight minute walk away from an area where another one of Charles Henry's relations lived, in Pound Lane, as we will mention later on in this book.

Charles, Charles Henry's cousin, married Annie Bennett on the 1st January 1867 in Brisbane, Australia[263], the place where his brother George Back Cutbush lived and passed away in. He, himself passes away on 31st December 1895 in Burwood, New South Wales, Australia[264].

...

---

[262] Kentonline.co.uk.
263 Marriage Record.
264 Death Record.

Number 24 St Margaret's Street in Canterbury today, (above) where Charles Henry's cousin worked before moving to Australia. ©Amanda Harvey Purse

Inside Number 24 in 1899 (right) from the author's collection.

Back to George's parents, *William and Elizabeth Cutbush, who were Charles Henry's uncle and aunt*, by 1841 we discover that William was a hairdresser in Highgate, Hawkhurst[265] and four years later, the couple have another child that they name her Mary Ann Cutbush[266], baptising her on the Christmas Eve of 1845 in Tonbridge[267].

Mary later becomes a Schoolmistress with her husband being the Schoolmaster at a school named Coft in Pakenham, Suffolk[268], eventually passing away in 1879[269].

One month after the birth of George Back Cutbush, we sadly find George's father, William, in debt to his father, James Cutbush and Henry Elgar, a Grocer from Ashford.

Although the amount of money owned was not noted, William had to 'assign all his real and personal Estates and Effects'[270] over to both men.

A hard task we can imagine for any family, let alone one with a new born and possibly made worse by knowing one of the creditors was your own father.

By 1851, William's fortunes had changed as he now owned a hairdresser's shop in the High Street of Tonbridge as this is stated on the census of that year.

---

[265] 1841 Census.
[266] She marries Henry James Bourne on the 8th October 1867 on St Leonard's in Hythe – Marriage Record. Their marriage being recorded in the local newspaper – Kentish Gazette - 15th October 1867. After the death of his wife, Henry remarries in 1881 to Sarah Henrietta Mitchell in St Giles, London – Marriage Record.
[267] Baptism Record.
[268] 1871 Census.
[269] In Suffolk – Death Record.
[270] Kentish Gazette - 21st May 1839.

However, we know that William was living in Tonbridge at least a year earlier than this as he appears within a long list of other people living there that were not happy with the act of 'betting on the races' coming to their town.

According to this list of people, betting and gambling on horses was an act of 'evil'[271].

William and his wife stayed in Tonbridge for forty years[272], when by 1891 he and his wife retired to Hythe, to live in Park Road[273], where he had also been appointed Special Constable of the town in the October of 1862[274][275].

One wonders, did Charles Henry knew of this role that his uncle had, considering Charles Henry was living in Hythe at the time?

If he did, can we then question whether this was Charles Henry's reason to want to join the police force himself or even to think that this was an option open for him to choose?

Could we then push this suggestion further and wonder if his 'Uncle William from Kent' was proud of his 'young nephew Charles Henry' for having a police career, later on?

All thought-provoking questions that at the very least, hopefully, makes us think past the simple fact that Charles

---

[271] Maidstone Journal and Kentish Advertiser - 16th July 1850.
[272] 1851 – 1891 Censuses.
[273] Described as retired on the 1891 Census.
[274] Kentish Gazette - 28th October 1862.
[275] Kentish Gazette 1904.

Henry joined the Metropolitan Police force on a certain date.

It can make us question what his family may have thought of his decision and that in turn can make us think of Charles Henry as the role he played within his family rather than instantly thinking of him as a policeman.

...

The address that William and his wife move to in Park Road still exists and it is a few minutes' walk away from the main high street of Hythe, on the other side of the river.

Today, there are still a few nuggets of history that the Cutbush's would have seen in the form of small, bricked Victorian houses along one side of the street, while amongst the other side now stands slight more modern buildings that were built by the 1970's.

Park Road is also very interesting when looking at its connections to the Cutbush family. As not only do members of this family live in this road at some point within their lives but at one end of this road it attaches itself to Stade Street, an address that we will see the Cutbush's would also have known very well for a number of different reasons.

Number 53 Stade Street in Hythe, today. ©Amanda Harvey Purse.

The Author outside Number 53 Stade Street in Hythe, the address Charles Henry's uncle retired to.

In 1901 we see William living at Number 53 Stade Street in Hythe[276.] William Cutbush passes away just three years later, on the 31st January 1904 in his 90th year[277].

He was buried originally in the family plot of 371 within the grounds of Hythe Congregational church, in the centre of that town.

If we wanted to visit this family plot in this church today, sadly we are not able to as in the 1980's this church was knocked down including all the headstones.

However, we are lucky that before this was done, a group of volunteers wrote down the inscription that had appeared on William's headstone and this was how we now know this was a family plot. As it stated this,

'In loving memory of William Henry Cutbush beloved son of William and Elizabeth, who departed this life on December 17th 1861 aged 24. In loving memory of Elizabeth Cutbush (wife of William Cutbush) who departed this life on December 28th 1897, aged 85 years. Also, William Cutbush, son to James and Lucy Cutbush, who departed this life 1904'[278].

...

Completing William Cutbush's life here we turn back to *James and Lucy, Charles Henry's grandparents* whose next child was, *Charles Cutbush* and as this is the line that eventually leads us to Charles Henry, we will leave this

---

[276] 1901 Census.
[277] Canterbury Journal, Kentish Times and Farmers' Gazette - 20th February 1904.
[278] Hythe Congregational Church records.

child for a moment and keep on the same family branch of its tree first, before stepping down to another one.

James and Lucy next have *Catherine Cutbush, Charles Henry's aunt*, and she born in 1819 in Kennington, being baptised on the 9th April 1819 in Parish Church in Kennington[279].

She married Jeffery Barton[280] on 28th August 1840 in St Mildred church in Canterbury[281]. Her husband had been married before to a Mary Ann Brown in Hampstead, London[282].

However, she had passed away in 1836 in Dover, Kent[283]. Jeffery and his second wife then have their first child, Jeffery Junior, a year after their marriage[284].

In 1841 the couple were living in New Street in Ashford Kent[285], this was just one out of a few addresses the family had lived in, as they also lived in the village of Brabourne, in Walnut Grove in Wye, Marsh Lane in Ashford and Castle Street in Ashford. [286]

After they had moved to New Street, an address we have mentioned before and this highlights another relation living

---

[279] Birth and Baptism Records.
[280] Born in 1812 in Dover – Birth Record. Baptised on 5th February 1812 in the church of St Mary the Virgin in Dover – Baptism Record.
[281] Marriage Record.
[282] Marriage Record.
[283] Death Record.
[284] Birth Record.
[285] 1841 Census.
[286] South Eastern Gazette - 7th October 1851.

in the area of Somerset Road, Jeffery was registered as a veterinary surgeon[287].

Also in 1841, Catherine gives birth to her second child and they name her Sarah Barton[288].

It is quite interesting to note that, on 16th February 1856, Jeffery Barton has two letters written to him in the Kentish Independent newspaper, congratulating him on his ointment of rat killer that he had designed[289].

That, in itself may not seem interesting, if we dismiss the fact that *Jeffery Barton was a vet and he had designed something to kill a type of animal*, however what makes these letters more interesting is, that one of them was written by James Clements, his brother in law, without ever mentioning that he was related to Jeffery.

Could this open the idea that this was the case of family self-advertising?

...

By 1861, the Barton family, had moved to Canterbury in New Bridge Street[290], while having to sell some of their horses, such as 'Bay Mare, 14 and half hands high, 8years old' and 'Brown Mare, 15 and half hands high' as well as two others.[291]

---

[287] 1841 Census.
[288] Birth Record.
[289] Kentish Independent - 16th February 1856.
[290] 1861 Census.
[291] South Eastern Gazette - 13th March 1860.

The reason for the selling of the horses could have been because Jeffery had struggled to pay the rent and a Mr White, collector of the said rent, had taken him to court over it. Jeffery however, had a bad case of gout at the time and could not attend the hearing[292].

Four years later his luck seemed to have turned, as he had gained a Veterinary surgery in Dover. We know this because on the 24th January 1869, Jeffery places an ad in the local newspaper, offering a job to a pupil willing to learn the trade of which he ends the ad by stating 'and will be treated as one of the family'[293].

Catherine passes away on the 19th February 1870, after which her husband moves his home address to Dover as well[294]. Jeffery passes away on 22nd February 1874 and both of them are buried in Canterbury City Cemetery, with other members of the Cutbush family, which will be mentioned later in this book.[295]

...

The next child James and Lucy were to have, was Ann Cutbush, who was baptised on 2nd November 1821 in the Parish Church of Kennington, Kent[296].

Ann, Charles Henry's aunt, married James Clements on 25th January 1849[297] in the same church Ann was baptised in.

---

292 Kentish Chronicle -25th March 1865.
293 Maidstone Journal and Kentish Advertiser - 30th January 1869.
294 Whitstable Times and Herne Bay Herald - 19th November 1870.
295 Death Records.
296 Baptism Record.
297 Marriage Record.

When they have their first child, James Cutbush Clements[298], they baptise him on the 3rd August 1851[299]. The next child Ann and James have was Emma Sarah Ann Clements[300], who they baptised on the 6th August 1854 in the Parish Church, Kennington[301].

Sadly, *Emma Sarah Ann Clements, Charles Henry's cousin* passes away on 2nd September 1932 inside Chartham Hospital, otherwise known East Kent Asylum at the age of seventy eight years[302].

This can be suggested as an important fact within the Cutbush family as we will be mentioning this and other connections *to this*, later on in this book.

By 1861 Ann and James were living with Amelia Cutbush, their great niece in Queen Street, Ashford[303] and from 1871 until Ann passes away, they live at Triangle Farm near Bybrook, James being registered as a farmer[304].

---

298 He later marries Emma Jane Crux (born 1854 Kennington – Birth Record) – Marriage Record. In 1871 the couple were living in Queens Street, Ashford. An address that has been mentioned before with other relations to the Cutbush family and an address not that far from Somerset Road – 1871 Census. On 25th February 1915, Emma passed away, with James passing away on 26th March 1927 – Death Records.
299 Baptism Record.
300 She lives with her parents at Triangle Farm by Bybrook, near Ashford – 1881 Census, until 1883, when she gave birth to Alexander Clements, father was unknown – Birth Certificate. By 1901 she was living in Parkstone in Dorset but by 1911 she was back near Ashford at Number 10 Lees Road, Willesborough – 1911 Census.
301 Baptism Record.
302 Death Record.
303 1861 Census.
304 1871 – 1891 Censuses.

Ann passes away on 22nd March 1891 in Willesborough, being buried in Willesborough parish church on 27th March 1891[305].

...

James and Lucy have another child in the summer of 1825, they name her Lucy Ellen Cutbush, baptising her on the 8th June 1825[306].

Lucy Ellen Cutbush, Charles Henry's aunt, married on the 18th September 1848 in the church of All Souls in Westminster, London[307]. She marries a Thomas Young Brockman[308] and by 1851 the couple were living at Number 22 Fairclough Lane in West Derby; her husband being registered as a clerk[309].

Ten years later, the couple were living at Number 185 Billbarn Road in Warwickshire and in 1871, they were living Coleman House, Claredon Road, Hertfordshire[310].

Lucy Ellen passed away in 1875 in Kensington, London, her husband passing away twenty years later in 1895[311].

---

305 Death and Burial Records.
306 Birth and Baptism Record.
307 Marriage Record.
308 He was born on 20th November 1825 in Dover, being baptised on 9th December 1825 in the church of St Mary the Virgin, Dover – Birth and Baptism Record. After Lucy, his wife dies, he remarries in the same year on 29th September 1875 in Old Church St Pancras – Marriage Record, he marries Margaret Alice McCormick (1843 – 1928) – Birth and Death Record.
309 1851 Census.
310 1861 and 1871 Censuses.
311 Death Records.

...

James and Lucy's last child was *James Cutbush, Charles Henry's uncle,* who was born in 1841[312] he grew up to be a seedman in Kennington, Kent.

By working as a seedsman, he, as well as his brother Charles, *Charles Henry's father*, had followed in the footsteps of their father, James Senior Cutbush. Who by this time was a recorded seedsman, a role of course other Cutbush relations had taken before them, as we have already mentioned in the book.

Lucy, Charles Henry's grandmother passed away in 1850 in Kennington, near Ashford and *James, Charles Henry's grandfather,* passed away on 25th May 1852, being buried on the 30th May 1852 in the Parish Church in Kennington[313], a funeral we can easy imagine, an eight year old Charles Henry, who lived nearby at the time, might have gone to.

We now turn back to Charles Henry's direct line of his family, through his father, Charles Cutbush.

---

[312] Birth Record.
[313] Death and Burial Records.

The Cutbush Connection

Charles Cutbush was born in 1816 to James and Lucy Cutbush and he was baptised on 17th November 1816 in the Parish church in Kennington[314].

His first child with his future wife, Amelia Stokes, was born to the couple in 1836 in the area of Broughton Aluph, near Ashford in Kent.

They name him, *Henry Cutbush, this would-be Charles Henry's only older brother,* and they baptism him on the 18th November 1836 in the Parish Church of Broughton Aluph[315].

On the 1841 census, we can see that this child was living with his grandparents on his mother's side in St Leonard's, Hythe, however ten years later, he was living with his parents in Ashford's main town[316].

Henry Cutbush married on the 31st May 1857, in the church of St Peters in Pimlico, London[317], he marries Eliza Pither[318] and their first child was born to them on 20th January 1858 in Westminster, London. They named her Amelia Cutbush[319] possibly named after Henry's mother.

---

[314] Birth and Baptism Record.
[315] Birth and Baptism Record.
[316] 1841 and 1851 Censuses.
[317] Marriage Record.
[318] Born 1838 in St George Hanover Square, London – Birth Record. In 1851 Eliza was living in the King's Head Public House in Hanover Square, with her father, William Pither being the landlord – 1851 Census.
[319] Birth Record.

This is the *Amelia, Charles Henry's niece,* we have mentioned before that was living with Ann and James Clements in Queens Street, Ashford, she was baptised on 27th January 1858 in the church of St John the Evangelist in Westminster, London.[320]

Charles and Amelia decide to marry in the year of 1838, they marry in the Parish Church called St Leonard's in Hythe on 4th May 1838[321].

Amelia Stokes was born in 1816 in Hythe[322], to Henry Stokes (1772 – 1857)[323] and Susannah Brazier (1791 – 1864)[324] and she was baptised on the 3rd April 1816[325] in the same church she later marries Charles Cutbush in.

...

St Leonard's church in Hythe, was a very important place for Charles Henry Cutbush's immediate family. This is because not only did his parents get married there, but we will see that his grandparents on his mother's side were buried there along with his own father and brother, John Love Cutbush. Also after the passing of Charles Henry, his mother would be buried there.

So, we can easily imagine that because of all this, at least, Charles Henry may have visited this church at one point in his life. With that in mind, the author felt she needed to visit the place for herself.

---

[320] Baptism Record.
[321] Marriage Record.
[322] Birth Record.
[323] Birth and Death Records.
[324] Birth and Death Records.
[325] Baptism Record.

...

Much like the rest of the town of Hythe, this church is situated on a side of a hill. Which means the graveyard surrounding the church slopes downwards towards the Kent seaside.

Although this can make it very difficult to visit if you are not the fittest of people as the slopes leading up to it *are not just steep but are very long*, it does set the scene for a lovely view once *and if* you get there.

The church still stands prominent in the town which shows us the importance of it from the days where it was a part of the pilgrim route to Canterbury Cathedral until now.

The church is also known for being one out of only two churches in England to have an Ossuary, a place where a large collection of preserved bones and skulls lay floor to ceiling in its crypt.

On the bright, sunny but perhaps a little windy day when the author visited it, the view from the church down to the sea was beautiful and peaceful. Making the author think that no wonder this church has been important to so many people over the many years it has stood there.

The author at St Leonard's Church at Hythe, where Charles Henry Cutbush's parents and sister married. It is also the place his grandparents, his parents, and his brother are buried.

The history that surrounds the church made it easy for the author to picture what it would have been like for the Cutbush's when they visited it for themselves.

We may also easily wonder how charming it is that the parents of the policeman that is the central character within this book, lays in their last resting place in such a location like the one in the church in Hythe.

…

As Henry and Susannah Stokes are the parents to Amelia Cutbush, which means they would have been Charles Henry's grandparents on his mother's side, perhaps we should spend a few moments getting to know them first, before moving on to other members within the family.

The Stokes

Henry Stokes was born in 1772[326] to Richard Stokes (baptised on 23rd October 1737 [327]in the church, his grandson in law, Charles Cutbush, later marries his granddaughter) and Mary Laker[328], who marry on the 30th October 1762 in the Parish Church in Hythe[329].

These would have been Charles Henry's Great Grandparents on his mother's side of the family.

Henry, was not the only child Richard and Mary were to have, they also had William Stokes, born in 1763, Thomas Stokes, born in 1765, Mary Stokes, born 1768, John Stokes, born 1770, then there was Ann Stokes, born 1774 and finally Elizabeth Stokes, born 1776[330].

All these people would have been Charles Henry's Great uncles and aunts on his mother's side.

Before Henry married Charles Henry's grandmother, he married Margaret Marshall on 15th May 1792 in Hythe.[331]

She was born in 1776 in Kent[332] and had one child with Henry before they married, this was John Stokes, born in 1792[333].

---

326 Birth Record.
327 Baptism Record.
328 Born 1740 – Birth Record.
329 Marriage Record.
330 Birth Records.
331 Marriage Record.
332 Birth Record.
333 Birth Record.

This would have been Charles Henry's step – uncle.

The couple carry on having more children after they married, with Edward Stokes being born in 1794, Mary Ann Stokes, born in 1796, Margaret Stokes, born in 1797, Ann Stokes, born in 1799 and Caroline Stokes, born in 1801[334].

Sarah Stokes was next, born in 1802, Rebecca Elizabeth Stokes, born in 1805, Richard Winter Stokes born 6th March 1806, who sadly dies on 23rd December 1806, Richard Thomas Stokes, born in 1807, who sadly dies a year later and *finally* Eliza Winter Stokes, born in the April 1810, she too sadly dies before the end of the year[335].

These would all have been Charles Henry's Step- aunts and uncles.

We can now see that Henry and his first wife had to deal with a number of deaths of their later children. With knowing this as well as knowing the actual amount of children Henry's wife gave birth too, it is perhaps not unexpected to find out that Henry's wife, passes away just two years after the birth of her eleventh child, her passing being on 23rd January 1812[336].

…

A year later Henry remarries *Susannah Brazier, Charles Henry's Grandmother,* on the 28th September 1813 at St Mary's in Northgate, Canterbury[337].

---

[334] Birth Records.
[335] Birth and Death Records
[336] Birth and Death Records.
[337] Marriage Record.

Sadly, only a part of this church that we see today would have been like it was when Charles Henry's grandparents married there[338]. This is because a part of it that was rebuilt in 1830, so when we look at it today we would see a mixture of different designs in one church, including a roman wall.

Also, St Mary's is actually not that far away from Canterbury City Cemetery where other members of Charles Henry's family were buried.

Susannah was born in 1791 in the area of St Margaret's, Kent, she was baptised in the church of St Margaret's at Cliffe, Kent[339].

This quiet Kentish town was rich in history, from farming lands to being a small fishing town and the occasional smuggling adventure.

Maybe because of the beauty of the town or the history that was attached to it, many famous people has lived there such Peter Ustinov, Noel Coward and even the James Bond writer Ian Fleming[340].

---

[338] Canterbury Archives.
[339] Birth and Baptism Record.
[340] St Margaret's – History.

St Mary's Church Northgate in Canterbury today. This is the church Charles Henry's grandparents on his mother's side married in, on 28th September 1813. This is also the church that Charles Henry's sister, Cassandra, marries in fifty seven years later. ©Amanda Harvey Purse.

**A postcard showing the church in which Charles Henry's grandmother of his mother's side, got baptised in, in the year of 1791.
From the author's collection.**

Henry and Susannah have *Eliza Stokes, Charles Henry's aunt,* born in 1814[341] and then two years later, Henry and Susannah *have Amelia Stokes in 1816, she would be the mother to Charles Henry Cutbush*[342].

By 1841, Henry was registered as a tailor living with his second wife and his grandson, (from Amelia, Charles Henry's mother) Henry Cutbush. They were living in Stade Street, Hythe, an address we have mentioned before with the Cutbush family.

Ten years later, Charles Henry's Grandparents, Henry and his wife Susannah, are running the St Bartholomew Alms in the High Street of Hythe.

St Bartholomew Alms was a place of residence for older persons, with set times that they must be home, otherwise they would have been locked out of their home.

The Stokes were living there with their granddaughter, Amelia (from Amelia, their daughter)[343].

Henry, Charles Henry's Grandfather on his mother's side, passes away on the 14th July 1857 and was buried in the Parish Church in Hythe on 20th July 1857.

This was the same church his daughter, Amelia had married Charles Cutbush nineteen years previously.

---

341 Birth Record.
342 Birth Record.
343 1841 and 1851 Census.

A postcard of the St Bartholomew Alms in the High Street of Hythe from the author's collection.

Back to
The Cutbush Connection

Charles and Amelia have their second child, Amelia in 1840, they baptised her on 21st June 1840 in the Parish Church in Kennington, near Ashford in Kent[344].

She, as we have already stated with living with her grandparents in 1851.[345] She marries on the Christmas Day of 1866 to James Stebbing in the Wesleyan Chapel in Elham[346].

James was born in 1837[347] in Mildenhall, Suffolk to Charles Stebbing (1809 – 1841)[348] and Elizabeth Copping (1800 – 1880)[349]. He had three siblings, Elizabeth Stebbing born in 1840, Sophia Stebbing born in 1833 and finally, Charles Stebbing born 1835[350].

James Stebbing becomes a Freemason of the Ancient Order of Foresters Court of St Leonards, Number 2350[351].

The origins of Ancient Order of Foresters are in the medieval idea of forest court, with Adam being the first forester.

Its aims are to be virtuous in all aspects of your life. It wasn't until 1892 that female members were allowed to

---

344 Birth and Baptism Record.
345 1851 Census.
346 Marriage Record.
347 Birth Record.
348 Birth and Death Records.
349 Birth and Death Records/
350 Birth Records.
351 Freemason Records.

join, which meant the emblem of the Order had to change to include a female figure[352].

Amelia and James have their first child, Elizabeth Olive Stebbing (1867 – 1931[353]) and a year later they have, Louisa Amelia Stebbing (1868 – 1955[354]) with their third child, who they called Charles Henry, (*possibly named after Amelia's brother, the person who becomes a policeman later on*) Stebbing (1870 – 1956)[355] coming along two years later.

...

In the 1871 census, it shows us that *Amelia, Charles Henry's older sister,* and James was living in Stade Street.

One of the many family photographs, the author has been able to see, shows Amelia standing outside her home with a shoe shop sign to the left of her.

This is a wonderfully piece of history here, as the Stebbing family ran a shoe fixing business from their home, a home they lived in for the next thirty nine years and the author was so lucky to have been able to see this little nugget of history.

The next children Amelia and James were to have was James Stebbing (1874 – 1961)[356] and Percy John Stebbing

---

[352] Freemasons Museum – History.
[353] Birth and Death Records.
[354] Birth and Death Records.
[355] Birth and Death Records.
[356] Birth and Death Records.

born in 1874[357], *all of these children would have been Charles Henry's nephews and nieces.*

Amelia and her husband, James, pass away in the same year of 1919 in Hythe, Kent[358].

...

If we go back to Amelia's parents, Charles and Amelia, we will see in 1841 for some reason Amelia was still registered as a 'Stokes' and not living with her husband. She was living within Bybrook House, near Ashford at the age of twenty two[359].

Charles, meanwhile appears to be living in the 'Church houses' (maybe he was not allowed to be married, or have his wife with him, while living there) in Wivelsfield, Chailey, Sussex and he was working as a Railway Labourer[360].

Amelia and Charles have another child in 1842, they name her Ellen Cutbush and baptised her on 4th May 1842 in the church of St Mary's in the main town of Ashford[361].

Ellen, Charles Henry's sister, gives birth to Florence Hastings (1860 - 1879) in Hythe[362] and a year later, on the 1861 census, she was *claiming, (*although no marriage

---

[357] Birth and Death Records.
[358] Death Record.
[359] 1841 Census.
[360] 1841 Census.
[361] Birth and Baptism Records.
[362] Birth Record.

record has been found to date) to be married while living in Newington, Surrey[363].

She next gives birth to Albert Henry Hastings in 1862 in Hythe[364]. She finally marries on 1st April 1865 in St Leonard's, Hythe[365].

However, she does not marry a Mr. Hastings as we may expect from the naming of her two children, she actually marries a man named John Trestain (1844 – 1921)[366].

By 1871, Ellen and her husband were living at Number 9 Newcastle Street in Staffordshire, where the couple were running a Confectioners[367].

By the time Ellen and her husband had moved to live in Swain Hotel in West Somerset, Ellen's children had been given to Ellen's mother, Amelia, (Charles Henry's mother) to look after[368].

Could we suggest that this happened because her husband, John did not want to bring up children that wasn't his own?

Of course, without knowing the family situation at this point, it will probably be always difficult to know for sure but it is a reasonable suggestion to think about as we carry on.

---

363 1861 Census.
364 Birth Record.
365 Marriage Record.
366 Birth and Death Record.
367 1871 Census.
368 1871 and 1881 Censuses.

Ellen passes away on the 4th September 1889 in Burnham, Somerset[369]. Ellen left her husband the sum of £235[370].

...

The next child Charles and Amelia were to have was **Charles Henry Cutbush**, this would be the man that would become a policeman for the Metropolitan Police force in London and be involved in the investigation case of 'Jack the Ripper', *however we of course will mention him and his family in more detail, later in this book.*

We know that at the time of Charles Henry's birth, his father was still working for *his* father, James Cutbush on James's land in Kennington. We know this because both son and father were mentioned in the local paper on 16th March 1844.

Thomas Holtum had been brought to court over stealing property from James Cutbush, the property was a sack of wheat from James's land.

In court James stated that he was,

'A seedman at Kennington and on the 6th January, he had some brown wheat mixed with velvet white in his granary.' [371]

A sack of wheat had previously ripped open and had emptied its contents on the floor, James had not got around to cleaning this before the other sack was stolen, so he was able to see footprints that wasn't his own and followed

---

369 Death Record.
370 Probate.
371 Canterbury Journal, Kentish Times and Farmers' Gazette - 16th March 1844.

them across the fields to Thomas Holtum's home. James had employed Thomas on several occasions so knew of his footprints[372].

Isn't this a wonderful picture we have here of Charles Henry's grandfather, as he follows clues, following the footprints across the fields to the criminal's home, like a certain fictional detective[373].

Could we even allow ourselves to wonder is this where Charles Henry got his policeman's mind from?

Whatever the answer is, this is a wonderful piece of family history, an event we did not know of and it makes the people we are researching a bit more human than just mentioning their names and dates.

In the same article we can see that *Charles, Charles Henry's father*, was also called to court to give evidence and in his statement, we find that James was not alone following the footprints like a detective, for his son, Charles was also doing the same.

It was Charles that goes off to fetch a policeman, a PC William Howell and returned with him to search 'the prisoner's home'.

On searching the home, they found a sack of wheat of which James '(who said he had been a seedman for forty years) examined the seeds and stated that they matched his

---

[372] Canterbury Journal, Kentish Times and Farmers' Gazette - 16th March 1844.
[373] Sherlock Holmes written by Sir Arthur Conan Doyle.

own. The prisoner was found guilty and sentenced to one year's imprisonment with hard labour'[374].

...

Charles Henry's younger sister was Cassandra Jeater (named after her grandmother's maiden name on her father's side of the family) *Cutbush*, born to Charles and Amelia in the latter quarter of 1845. She was baptised on 2nd January 1846 in the main church in the town of Ashford called St Mary's[375].

Cassandra married on the Christmas Day of 1870 to John Shurbsole Denne, a Gas Fitter at that time, in the same church her grandfather had married her grandmother on her mother's side of the family, in St Mary's in Northgate, Canterbury, with her sister Alice being a witness[376].

John was born in 1844 in Canterbury, being baptised on the 7th July 1844 in the Parish church[377]. By 1851 John was living in Barnham, Kent, ten years later he was back in Canterbury[378], where he met Cassandra.

By 1871, Cassandra was living with her husband and father in law, at St Radigumde Street in Canterbury[379]. Ten years later, the couple were living on their own at Number 39 Castle Row, Canterbury.

---

374 Canterbury Journal, Kentish Times and Farmers' Gazette - 16th March 1844.
375 Birth and Baptism Record.
376 Marriage Record.
377 Birth and Baptism Record.
378 1851 and 1861 Censuses.
379 1871 Census.

This is an address that still exists today, of which a business is run from.

However, because they have kept the original Victorian front[380], we can still see what the house looked like when Cassandra and her husband lived there.

Cassandra was heavily pregnant at this time as she gives birth to her first child in the December of that same year.

They name him after his father, John Shrubsole Denne, sadly John Junior was to pass away at the age of just ten years old, on 3rd April 1882.

He was buried in Canterbury City Cemetery; his memorial ID number is 169563045.[381]

In June of 1873, Cassandra and John were to have another child, who they name Albert Denne, they baptised him on 6th July 1873[382].

He later joins the army on 2nd March 1915 being Private 200934 in the East Kent Regiment called The Buffs[383]. He gets discharged, due to sickness, on 7th May 1919[384].

---

380 1881 Census.
381 Canterbury City Cemetery records.
382 Baptism Record.
383 Canterbury City Cemetery records.
384 Silver War Badge Records.

Number 39 Castle Row in Canterbury today. The home of Cassandra Denne, Charles Henry Cutbush's sister. ©Amanda Harvey Purse.

Although he receives a Silver War Badge on the 7th June 1919[385], sadly, Albert passed away on 6th November 1919, aged forty six years old.

His war grave is in Section Grave 200 in Canterbury City Cemetery, he lies next to his parents and brother and sister[386].

His headstone was paid by his younger brother, a Mr. Charles Denne, who at the time of his brother's death was living at Number 71 Pound Lane, Canterbury[387].

…

In 1881, John Sr was a house painter and all children that were old enough, were school, while Cassandra's occupation was left blank on all census.[388]

The couple made one final move to Number 24 Pound Lane, Canterbury, by 1891. They would stay in this property until they both pass away later on.

Sadly, this building, unlike Castle Row, does not exist anymore, in fact Pound Lane stops at Number 23 today and next to it, is a dusty unused piece of land, when the author visited it.

This is because the road flooded out both on October 1909, when Cassandra and her husband still lived there and once more on the day after Boxing Day in 1927, destroying some of the homes along it.

---

385 Silver War Badge Records.
386 Canterbury City Cemetery records.
387 War graves records.
388 1881 Census.

This means today, the numberings seem a little odd to us in Pound Lane as the numbers go in order rather than normally skipping a number[389].

In 1891 Cassandra and John have their son, Albert, at the age of seventeen being a blacksmith and living with them.

Charles (born 1876[390]) their son, was a shoemaker and all their other children, Richard (born 1878[391]), Harry (born 1880[392]), Ellen Amelia (born 1882[393]), Cassandra (born 1883[394])and Annie (born 1887[395]), were at school[396].

All of these children would have been Charles Henry Cutbush's nephews and nieces.

In 1901, the Denne family were still living at Number 24 Pound Lane. John was a Plumber's Clerk, their son Albert was registered as a shoemaker, like their other son Charles was also.

'Harry' now becomes Henry on this census and was a cycle engineer and all the other children were at home with an added family member, in the form of Albert Junior, born in 1899, who was the grandson of Cassandra and John, this also *makes Albert Junior, Charles Henry's great nephew*[397].

---

[389] Historical Canterbury – History of Pound Lane.
[390] !891 Census.
[391] 1891 Census.
[392] 1891 Census.
[393] 1891 Census.
[394] 1891 Census.
[395] 1891 Census.
[396] 1891 Census.
[397] 1901 Census.

Ten years later, the family are still living at Number 24 Pound Lane, Albert and Charles are still shoe makers and Richard seems to have joined them in their careers.

Cassandra Junior, recorded as 'Cassy' is at home with her parents as well as the grandson Albert, who was at school[398]

Cassandra Denne's husband passes away in the April of 1916, being buried in Canterbury City Cemetery.

…

On 30th October 1921, we can see a Cassandra Jeater Denne was having her banns read at Holy Cross Church in Canterbury so that she could marry, William Rose[399].

This would suggest at first, that Cassandra nee Cutbush was remarrying, however looking in to this a little deeper, we actually find it was the daughter, Cassandra Jeater Denne, who was marrying William Rose.

We know this because, this daughter was buried with her mother in 1968, at the age eighty four, under the name Cassandra Jeater Denne Rose[400].

In the January of 1923, *Cassandra Denne, Charles Henry's sister*, passes away. She was buried with her husband in Section Grave Number 184[401].

---

398 1911 Census.
399 CCA/U3/10/1/15 – Canterbury Cathedral Archives.
400 Canterbury Grave Records.
401 Death and Burial Records.

Her son, Charles, passed away in 1959 and he was buried near his parents in plot A Grave 429 in Canterbury City Cemetery[402].

Her other son, Harry or Henry Denne passed away in April of 1940, at the age of sixty one, was buried in the same cemetery, however he was buried plot Q grave 19[403].

...

As so many of this side of the Cutbush/Denne family were buried at Canterbury City Cemetery, the author thought it was only right for her to visit them, considering Cassandra was Charles Henry's younger sister.

With getting some help at Canterbury Cemetery staff[404], the author managed to find Cassandra's last resting place and amazingly, she has a headstone.

This thrilled the author so much, as after her many trips to many different cemeteries over the years for research, it is very common for her to not find a headstone or even some sort of marker. So many people just disappear in layers of grass and mud and for the author, at least, that also means so their history disappears also[405].

---

[402] Canterbury Grave Records.
[403] Canterbury Grave Records.
[404] The author would like to thank Terry at Canterbury Cemetery, it was getting close to his shift ending when I met him but he still kindly took the time to show me Cassandra and family grave.
[405] Although the author fully accepts that she can't put a headstone on every grave plot that doesn't one, she will still try her best to do what she can for as many people as she can. By writing books of their history and with people like you, the reader, to read it, hopefully these people won't have quite have disappeared as much.

However, this is not the case with Cassandra and her family. To know that Charles Henry's sister, nieces and nephews have a headstone really did mean a lot to the author, especially as we will see later in this book that headstones can not always be used for this family.

The grave was surrounded by kerb sets which have the faded names of both Cassandra and her husband, John written of them.

There was a cross placed in the middle of the grave and although, the cross has broken away from its block and lays across the grave, the name of Richard and Cassandra can be seen at the base.

Albert's war grave, as mentioned before, sits beside his family and the other members of the family are not that far away either.

Considering there was road was just over a fence and feet away from the graves, it still seemed a very peaceful and calm place to be.

The author felt like she would have stayed there for hours, being protected by the over grown trees and just hearing nothing but birds having conversations with each other.

...

Author at Canterbury City Cemetery, where quite a few of Charles Henry's close relations are buried.

Canterbury City Cemetery.
©Amanda Harvey Purse

The child Charles and Amelia have next was *Richard Brazier* (named after his grandmother's maiden name on his mother's side) *Cutbush, Charles Henry's younger brother*.

Richard was born in 1847 in Ashford, being baptised on 6th August 1847 in the church of St Mary's in the main town[406]. However, he was sadly, later buried in the same year, on 10th August 1847 in Gouldhurst, Kent.

Charles Henry Cutbush would have been three years old at the time of his younger brother's passing. Would he have known?

Would he have understood?

Did he know something was wrong but couldn't understand what that something was?

All reasonable suggested questions for us to think about, now we are looking at Charles Henry in a different, perhaps more human way.

---

[406] Birth and Baptism Records.

Author at the grave of Charles Henry's sister and her family, Cassandra Jeater Denne née Cutbush in Canterbury.

Charles Henry's sister's name written on her grave. 'Cassandra Jeater Denne'. ©Amanda Harvey Purse.

Charles Henry's nephew, Albert Denne's War Grave, next to his mother, Cassandra. ©Amanda Harvey Purse.

On 26th February 1849, Charles Henry's father and his uncle Frederick was coming back to Ashford from Kennington on a pony and cart, when they met with an accident.

The pony collapsed, causing both brothers to fall forward and land on the road. Frederick was not hurt, however Charles had 'severely lacerating the head and face'. He was carried home and a surgeon was called, he recovered, just leaving scars upon his head and face[407].

What an interesting piece of information we have found here, because without knowing of this accident, we may not have pictured Charles, Charles Henry's father, with scars upon his face. This makes Charles Cutbush more human than just a name or even the title of 'Superintendent Charles Henry Cutbush's father'.

This is also an interesting fact, because it mentions scars being on a person we are researching. As well as this making them perhaps more human to our picture of them, scars being on a person we are researching, almost repeats itself, albeit not on his face, later on in Charles Henry's own leavers file in the Metropolitan Police force.

…

Two years later, Charles and Amelia have *John Love Cutbush, Charles Henry's brother*, in 1849. However, he sadly passes away in 1858 and would be buried with his father in Hythe at a later date[408].

---

407 South Eastern Gazette - 27th February 1849.
408 Birth and Burial Records.

A year later Charles and Amelia have their next child, Percy Cutbush in the third quarter of 1850, baptising him on 25th September 1850 in the church of St Mary. However, he would visit that church soon after, as he sadly does not live the year out and was buried just four days after his baptism, on 29th September 1850.[409].

Charles and Amelia's next child was named *Alice Maud Cutbush, Charles Henry's sister*, she was born in 1851 in Ashford, however she did not get baptised until 6th May 1860 in Hythe[410].

By 1871, she had moved to Farnham, Aldershot to be working as a servant at the age nineteen[411].

...

In 1851, this side of the Cutbush family were living above a shop that they also owned in the High Street in the Ashford, the shop they ran was a Florist. *Amazingly, again we are seeing another side to the same Cutbush family working with flowers.*

Charles, as we have already mentioned was a seedman, but by this time he was owning land on the boarder of Ashford in Woodchurch and Sevington[412] to grow his seeds, Dutch bulbs and Russian Mats.

They were then stored in a warehouse at the back of the George Inn in the High Street of Ashford, not far away

---

409 Birth, Baptism and Burial Records.
410 Birth and Baptism Record.
411 1871 Census.
412 Kentish Gazette - 24th August 1852.

from his own premises, to sell inside the shop and on a stall in Corn Market, Canterbury[413].

By 1852, we can see that Charles Cutbush had tried to make his business a success in London, as he resides at 'the New Inn, Westminster Bridge Road, Lambeth and late of No.48 Hercules Buildings, Westminster Road in the Parish of St Mary, Lambeth, Surrey'[414].

However, we find this statement because of an event that could not be described as a lucky one, Charles was claiming insolvency of his business[415].

The Cutbush family have one more child, who they name Albert Cutbush in the third quarter of 1853[416], he would later get baptised on the same day as his sister, Alice, on 6th May 1860 in Hythe[417]. Sadly, Albert[418] was not to get to know his father.

Charles Cutbush, Charles Henry's father passes away on the 19th May 1854 in Sandgate, Cheriton near Folkestone, Kent.

He was buried on 23rd May 1854, in Hythe within his son, John Love Cutbush's, grave[419].

---

413 Kentish Gazette - 24th August 1852.
414 Kentish Gazette - 24th August 1852.
415 Kentish Gazette – 24th August 1852.
416 Birth Record.
417 Baptism Record.
418 Albert would pass away on 19th September 1884 and at the time of his death he was living with his brother, Charles Henry, the policeman, at his address of Number 36 St Paul's Road, London. Albert leaves the sum of £67 to Charles Henry Cutbush – Probate.
419 Death and Burial Records.

In 1861 and after the death of her husband, Amelia takes her children and goes to live in Hythe. A town she would have known since she was a child.

She sets up home for her family in Chapel Street, not that far from Stade Street in Hythe, where her brother a law lived.

At this point, she is working to help keep the roof over the heads of her children as she listed as a Seamstress, she is widow and she is aged forty five years old[420].

...

Chapel Street in Hythe amazingly is still there for us to see today, which is made even more wonderful considering Amelia took her children, including one, Charles Henry Cutbush, to live there.

It is a little side street that runs around the back of the small church of St Michael's. It is also the road running behind the main high street, near the town hall and quite near the place where her parents had lived and worked, in the St Bartholomew Alms.

The river was also very close by to this address and perhaps we could allow ourselves to imagine a young Charles Henry visiting the river bank on a sunny day, when not working in the occupation that will be later mentioned.

This thought is mentioned only because it is not often, we researchers of the 1888 murders, can think of policemen

---

[420]1861 Census.

that had an involvement into that investigation, being young boys, enjoying life.

However, in the visit to Hythe and walking around the area that a young teenaged Charles Henry Cutbush would have known, that thought, was all that kept repeating itself to the author.

...

Ten years later, Amelia (under the name of Catbash rather than Cutbush) was actually living in the same street as her brother in law, the shoe fixer, at Number 53 Stade Street, Hythe[421].

However, Amelia does not stay in the town she would have known since her own childhood, for the next twenty years, Amelia lives with her son, Charles Henry, while he was working as policeman, in London[422].

She passes away and was buried on 15th January 1900 in St Leonard's Church in Hythe, her last address was given as Number 52 Stade Street[423].

Proving in the last years of her life, she had returned to Hythe, possibly after the death of her son, Charles Henry and perhaps to be near her husband that had passed away almost fifty years before her.

---

421   1871 Census.
422   1881 and 1891 Censuses.
423   Death Certificate.

The area in which Charles Henry's father, mother and brother are buried in Hythe. ©Amanda Harvey Purse.

Chapel Street in Hythe today. Where Charles Henry Cutbush lived before becoming a policeman. ©Amanda Harvey Purse.

We have now seen a few numbers of Stade Street having importance to various different levels of the Cutbush family.

With that being stated, the author felt it was necessary to visit the street for herself.

It is a very long street running from the bridge over the river, all the way down to the sea front. It was a little difficult in finding the right numbers to the houses that the Cutbush's once lived in. This is because of the odd numbering of the street.

Number 53 is situated at the end of the street, near the sea front of the left-hand side if you were to be facing the sea, while Number 52 is on the right-hand side about half way back along the road and nearer to the bridge and High Street of Hythe.

Number 52 Stade Street in Hythe, today. ©Amanda Harvey Purse.

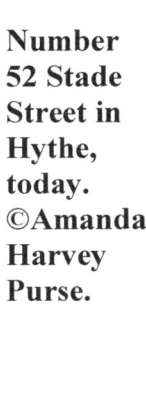

Author at Number 52 Stade Street in Hythe. Where Amelia, Charles Henry's mother, spent her last years.

Connections to
Charles Henry Cutbush

Now with knowing the very long and vast background to Charles Henry Cutbush, through his many relations, we can see a number of points that could be suggested to, make the man himself.

We know that the name Cutbush travels back to at least the 1700's. They were hard working, manual labourers, working with nature at all levels of their family tree, whether it be on farms, workhouse grounds, in nursery's, Florists or the Kentish fields.

They were people that were often strong willed, some wanting to make great success with their lives by moving away from what they had known. While others seemed to be drawn to certain areas and stayed there for the rest of their lives, becoming well known and even well liked in the villages they were a part of.

We have seen the highs of the family with the Highgate connection becoming well known for their nurseries, so much so that they were the eventual gardeners for the Royal Parks in London.

However, times were not always easy for them, success would also bring trouble, albeit with staff not behaving correctly or themselves being seen as bribers.

When Herbert Cutbush was called to court over the act of corruption, Herbert was recorded as stating 'very frankly' that he had done nothing wrong.

This could suggest a Cutbush that is strong willed, forceful in making his point and someone that does not like to have been suggested of wrongdoing.

This could also be suggested as being characteristics that may show themselves later with an event within Charles Henry's own life.

We have also seen the terrible, terrible lows for the family as a certain member did not live until their natural age limit. This member suffered with an illness that could be said to have been sadly, the reason they had taken their life.

What is similarly interesting when we are comparing family members' actions to Charles Henry, himself, is that with the Cutbush that sadly hanged himself, William, he had been in declining health leading up to his death, since an accident where he injured his right knee.

When looking at that event in this way, we can see a version of this history almost repeating itself later on.

This is also a great example of where looking into the family trees of a person can give us a more rounded view of that said person we are researching themselves, as sadly this was not the only time where a life ended perhaps too soon.

Sticking with this William Cutbush, it was also stated in the newspapers that were mentioning his death, that he felt the loss of his wife 'keenly'.

As we now know, this was not the first wife to pass away before him and for the newspaper to mention this, could it suggest that it was obviously known that William had changed a little? Maybe he was a little, what we would call, depressed?

Certainly, his ending seems to suggest this too and it is interesting to see that William seems to have been not alone in his turning to depression within his family as we will see later on.

...

Within this subject we also have Charles Henry's cousin, Emma Sarah Ann Clements. Who, it is quite possible that Charles Henry would have known, at least in his early childhood.

He would have been ten years old when she was born and the place in which her parents lived, in Queens Street, Ashford, would have been within a two-minute walk away from him at the time.

Emma ended her days on the 2nd September 1932 inside Chartham's St Augustine's Hospital, otherwise known as East Kent Asylum[424].

This hospital was first opened in 1875 in Maidstone, Kent, however it was not long before it was not large enough to house all the patients needed to stay there, a new place had to be found.

---

[424] This is also the same place Inspector Reid's, who would also be a part of the Jack the Ripper investigation, wife would end her days, thirty two years before Emma Clements – for more information please see Inspector Reid: The Real Ripper Street by Amanda Harvey Purse.

At the time Emma would have stayed there, the hospital would have also been used for the Second World War Emergency Medical Service[425].

However, what is perhaps more noteworthy to this Cutbush family story is that the hospital had been in the news in the 1970's when a nurse called Barbara Bishop received an MBE after she risked her own life to save a *suicidal* patient there[426].

With that being stated, we now know that Emma was in a place that dealt with sadly people who may have wished to end their own life.

This suggests at least two family members to Charles Henry who have connections to the very sad case of suicide, something that has not been mentioned before when discussing Charles Henry or his actions later on.

…

This may give us a new, if not different view, to events that were to come in the policeman's life and maybe with knowing this now we can think a little deeper about the very sad moment, when it comes and is later mentioned in this book.

There is always a life before a death and nobody should be defined by their death alone, so we will of course discuss the life of Charles Henry Cutbush.

---

[425] History of a hospital (St Augustine's Hospital Chartham) in Bygone Kent – R. Allen 1990.
[426] The Times - 10th December 1969.

However, before we do, we should perhaps discuss a little matter that we mentioned at the beginning of this book. A matter that could be suggested as consuming the reason why Charles Henry often gets mentioned with the Jack the Ripper case.

We have just gone through the very vast family tree of Charles Henry Cutbush, we have met interesting characters that have sat within its branches.

We have not only focused on a generation back from Charles Henry, but a further generation back from there and in some cases, one more from there. We have not just mentioned Charles Henry's siblings but have mentioned their children also.

We have met Great Great Grandparents, Great Grandparents and Grandparents on both sides of his family. We have met Great uncles and aunts, actual uncles and aunt and even step uncles and aunts, we have met cousins.

However, perhaps more importantly to some, we have met nieces and *nephews.*

…

At the beginning of this book we discussed the suggested pressures that researching the Cutbush family tree can bring, because of the nine little words Sir Melville Macnaghten of the Metropolitan Police force writes, when he was describing a suggested Jack the Ripper suspect, that being a Thomas Cutbush.

He states, 'Cutbush was the nephew of the late Supt. Executive'.

Now, this author can't tell you that Thomas Cutbush was Jack the Ripper, not because she disagrees with that opinion and not because she agrees with it either.

She can't tell you this because whoever you think was Jack the Ripper, *if you indeed agree on a suspect,* is yours and only yours to have.

Your opinion is your own and the fact that we sometimes have different opinions on things, makes for a healthy conversation and if we are talking about the history, for the author at least, she feels that this action is keeping history alive, which is perhaps more important in the large scheme of things.

She also can't tell you one hundred percent that Thomas Cutbush was or was not related to Charles Henry Cutbush.

This is because the author likes to play fair on both sides of an opinion and to do this she can't dismiss the document in which Sir Melville writes his nine little words in. She can't dismiss the fact that he wrote them and the possibility of his reasonings of doing so. She can't get out of her head that he must have had a reason to believe this was the case, whether that reason was correct or not.

Similarly, she can't dismiss the floating suggestion that Thomas was related through Charles Henry's mother's side of the family, with a (to date) non-recorded birth.

All she can tell you, is what you have just seen with her, in this book.

We have seen the recorded nephews of Charles Henry Cutbush and not only does there not seem to be a Thomas on this list, but the name of 'Thomas Cutbush' doesn't seem to appear much at all in Charles Henry's family tree, of which she feels, at least, we have dig deep into.

However, to play fair with this subject and to pay fair with you, the reader, she guesses we will have to wait for the day *if evidence appears for us all to see*, linking the two men together.

However, for right now, for today and for this book, all she can say to you is: She have come into this with an open mind, she have tried, she have dig deep, but she simply can't find the link for you.

Charles Henry Cutbush - Childhood

Charles Henry Cutbush was born to Charles and Amelia Cutbush on 5th January 1844, his mother registering him on the 3rd February 1844[427].

At time of his birth Charles Henry, was surrounded by siblings with his father working for his grandfather on the fields surrounding the town he would grow up in, in Ashford, Kent.

Ashford in Kent, has a curious history within itself. Jack Cade, who would go on to led a rebellion against King Henry the Sixth has been said to have come from Ashford.

This mainly comes from the fact in William Shakespeare's play Henry VI part two, Jack is seen talking to 'Dick, the butcher from Ashford'[428].

Also, Queen Elizabeth the First gave a manor house that was situated in Ashford to Thomas Smythe.

He was a Member of Parliament for Tavistock, Aylesbury, Rye, Winchelsea and Portsmouth over the years and his main role was to collect customs duties (taxes).

Thomas was buried in the same church as Charles Henry's relations were, in St Mary's Church, Ashford[429].

It was quite possible that Charles Henry's family were already living above the florist shop in the high street when

---

[427] Birth Certificate.
[428] Henry VI-part 2 Act 4 – William Shakespeare.
[429] History of Parliament online.

he was born, as already mentioned, possibly paying roughly forty pounds per annum[430] to do this.

...

The shop in with Charles Henry was born in still exists and wonderfully, although the shop has changed hands over the many years since the Cutbush's once owned it,[431] it has been a *Florist* for some time now.

To then know of this wonderful fact, that the person we are researching was born in a Florist shop and one hundred and seventy four years on the building, not only exists still but is actually a Florist shop, the author just had to visit the place.

To actually stand in the same building that the main character of this book was born in and to be surrounded by very beautiful looking flowers while I was in there was so touching.

History, was not only repeating itself but I felt for Charles Henry's history at least, it really did feel alive in that moment.

The building has had its own little slice of history, even before the Cutbush's had ever step foot inside. This was because Numbers 48 to 52 High Street was one large building once owned by Thomas Fenner in the 16th Century.

---

[430] In 1857 a butcher's shop with a house attached was going for that price in the High Street in Ashford near the Royal Oak Inn – South Eastern Gazette - 7th July 1857.

[431] Being a Butchers for example.

He passed it on to his son, John Fenner and upon his death in 1701, the building was then passed to his four daughters. Each one of his daughters divided the building up into four homes while keeping the same roof that connects all the numbers together[432], even today.

In an odd quirky fact, this meant that the roof under which Charles Henry Cutbush was born was first built over three hundred and forty years before himself.

Something we don't always think of when researching people and connecting them to the places they would have known.

Living in that building, meant that by the day of his christening, Charles Henry would have been carried out of the shop, possibly by his father, with his mother and siblings following behind.

They would have walked across the pebbled roadway of the busy high street and passed the Victorian water pump.

They would have been headed towards a little alleyway that was in between two buildings, while possibly hearing the bells of the church ring as they went.

---

[432] The author would like to thank Beth at Linda's Florist, for the conversations and the history and for going above and beyond by giving the details of the building and photographs of the area.

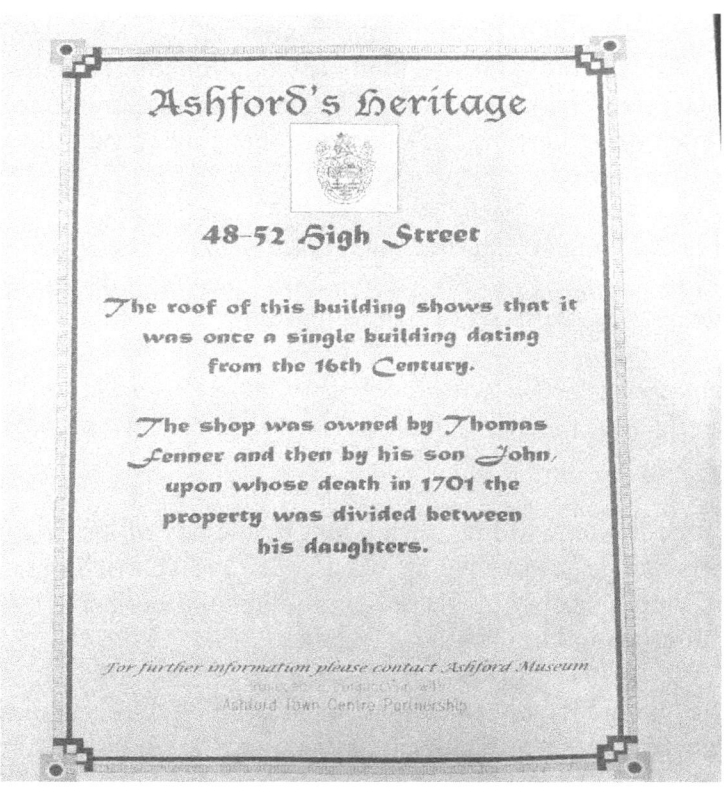

A part of the certificate found inside the premises of where Charles Henry Cutbush was born. The author would whole-heartily like to thank Linda's Florist for this.

The view from where Charles Henry was born to the church he was baptised in (above), showing the water pump from the author's collection.

The view from where Charles Henry was born to the looking towards where the church is that he got baptised in, at the time of writing (left) ©Amanda Harvey Purse

Maybe to set the scene even more in our heads, we can even allow ourselves to think that the young baby Charles Henry, hearing his older siblings play as they entered the churchyard.

...

The church is which Charles Henry Cutbush was baptised, St Mary's Church was built in the 13th Century, being added to by the 15th Century.

This remodelling was organized by John Fogg, a courtier, soldier and supporter of the Woodville family, under King Edward the fourth and who eventually, who fought against King Richard the third.

John Fogg was buried at the church and there is a memorial window still dedicated to him inside.[433]

The church of St Mary's was and still is situated in a form of a courtyard, with many small bowing houses to all sides. The courtyard has three entrances, two of which are quite small and one that was large enough to bring a horse and cart from one of the main roads to the side of the church.

Opposite the entrance to the church was the first Norton Knatchball School, in a building known as Dr Wilks' Hall, today it is now the building that houses Ashford's Museum.

---

[433] Notes of Brasses, Memorial Windows and Escutcheons Formerly Existing in Ashford and Willesborough Churches – Herbert L Smith 1859.

Author by the place Charles Henry was born in, in Ashford. Showing the connecting roof.

High Street in Ashford today. ©Amanda Harvey Purse.

Considering the closeness to where the Cutbush's were living at the time and to the school, that was for pupil's families that had not much money, it would be a reasonable suggestion that perhaps for a few years at least, Charles Henry might have gone there.

He would certainly have seen the pupils going in and leaving the school in his early days as he was living so close to school, as well as being amongst the busy life that living on a High Street of any town would bring.

For example, market day would have been on every first, third and fifth Tuesday of the month, this would have been a busy day for the town and with the market being just a few streets away from where Charles Henry was living with his family, we can presume he visited it, seeing all the animals being walked in, off the fields nearby[434].

Having all the shops, selling their wares on Charles Henry's door step, we can imagine a young boy, such as he was, looking into the shops fronts. Of which he had vast array of different items to view, from a Grocers shop, a butcher's, a dentist, a clothes maker to even a book printing company, all on the same street as his family's florist[435].

---

[434] Maidstone Journal and Kentish Advertiser - 13th April 1858.
[435] Maidstone Journal and Kentish Advertiser - 16th October 1858.

Photographs of Ashford, found in the premises of where Charles Henry was born in. Thanks to Linda's Florist for these photographs.

Charles Henry's family lived in the High Street from at least from 1841 to at least 1852, when the family then tried to make it in London for a short time before returning to the area.

This being stated, it was interesting to note that there is a bronze plague next-door to the building that Charles Henry was born in.

On this plague it states,

'In Memory of Henry Harrison 1811 – 1866. Plumber, Glazier and Painter. Inventor of The Water Pump 1841 signed in the presence of Queen Victoria, 4th March 1841'.

This is made even more a touching thought, when we consider there was indeed a water pump on the other side of the road from this building.

This not the only connection the town has to Queen Victoria. In 1898, the year after the Queen's diamond Jubilee, a seventeen-acre plot of farmland, that was originally called Banky Field, *a name probably how Charles Henry would have known the area to be*, was brought from a Mr George Elwick Jemmett and Mr Francis Bond Jemmett, whose names still appears on busy roads within Ashford.

The seventeen acres were renamed Victoria Park and the park still exists today, known to the locals as Vicky Park, it was officially opened in the July of 1899.

Although, it is wonderful to still have this Victorian park today, it sadly only has two Victorian landmarks left inside it.

The Grade Two listed Hubert Fountain was one of the landmarks. It was originally designed for the Second Great International Exhibition, held at the Horticultural Society Gardens in Kensington, London in the July of 1862.

In 1910 a Mr. George Harper brought the fountain and gave it to Victoria Park on one condition that every year on the 23rd July, his birthday, the fountain would be switched on and be celebrated. Something that still happens today.

The second landmark is the metal gates that are at one end of the park. The gates were a part of a metal fence that surrounded the park, however the fence is long gone, leaving only the gates behind, which were painted an odd blue colour a few years ago.

They were originally placed in the park in 1899 when the park opened and were first repainted in 1903 at the same time as the bandstand was, which sadly is no longer there[436].

---

[436] Victoria Park Conservation Plan – Ashford Borough Council.

Author at the Hubert Fountain in Victoria Park, today.

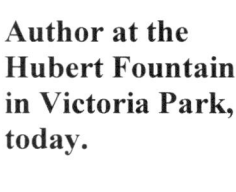

The Hubert Fountain in Victoria Park in Ashford. ©Amanda Harvey Purse.

The Victorian gates in Victorian Park ©Amanda Harvey Purse

Author at the gates in Victoria Park in Ashford.

...

As Charles Henry was growing up, he would have seen his family grow in considerable size, Cassandra Jeater Cutbush was born two years after him, then there was Richard Brazier Cutbush a year after that, plus there was also John Love Cutbush who was born in 1849.

By 1850, when Charles was only six years old, he had to cope with the second death of a close family member. Percy Cutbush was born in 1850, however he also passes away within the same year.

With that happening what can we imagine a young Charles Henry was thinking?

He was only six years old, did he now understand, more than he did with the first death, when he was only three years?

Did he wonder why this had happened as he had seen his mother give birth to other children before and yet some had survived while others had not?

We can imagine that his parents were distraught but with the father having to go back to work to pay for his existing family, did Charles Henry see the distress more in his mother?

The area is which Charles Henry's younger brother, Percy was buried at St Mary's Church, Ashford. (above) ©Amanda Harvey Purse.

A postcard of St Mary's Church in the author's collection.

Did this bring a closeness to them and is this why his mother, Amelia goes to live with Charles later on?

Of course, these are personal questions, so we will never really know the answers to them as so much time has passed, however that is not always the point of asking questions.

Sometimes, asking questions can make us think differently about an event or perhaps think a little more deeply about that event, of what it may mean to someone's life that we are researching.

For example, Percy's passing could have been stated in this book as a fact that happened, but with now asking these questions we can maybe now think differently about this event as Percy Cutbush wasn't just a name that we must mention because he was a part of Charles Henry's family tree.

He was Charles Henry's brother, he was Charles and Amelia Cutbush's son. He was the second death that Charles Henry had to cope with, within his close family at the tender age of just six years old and it was probably the first time that Charles Henry understood in some small way what a death can do to a family. Sadly, this would not be the only death he would see.

A year later Alice Maud Cutbush is born to the family, she would not be baptised until nine years later when the family had moved away from Ashford.

Could we then wonder if the reason behind this decision of not baptising her straight away was because Charles and Amelia not want to walk into the church, that was so close to them, with another child that now held their last resting place of their son Percy, so soon after his death?

This suggestion could have been a reasonable decision for anyone to make, with what the parents had been through.

...

In 1852, we already know Charles was trying his last attempt at making his business work in London as his addresses were stated as The New Inn on Westminster Bridge Road and Number 48 Hercules Buildings on Westminster Road.

We know that this attempt failed as he had to claim bankruptcy but did his family follow him to London for this short period of time?

If they did, was this then the first glimpse Charles Henry had of the capital at the age of eight years old?

What did the young Charles Henry think of it? Would he remember this moment when the time came for him to return to the busy streets of London?

Author outside St Mary's Church, Ashford. Where Charles Henry Cutbush was baptised and where members of his family are buried, including his younger brother.

Just two years later, another death happened for the Cutbush's and if they had thought the deaths of Richard and Percy was perhaps life changing, losing Charles Cutbush, the head of the household, must have been traumatic for many reasons.

Yes, Charles was Charles Henry's only father figure and we can imagine the emotion stings that, in itself can attach on to a young boy, losing his father.

However, there was also other issues that this must have caused as Charles Cutbush was also the main person that brought home money to feed his children.

This meant Amelia had to, because *she really had no choice*, step up and perhaps put her own grief to one side and become the father as well as the mother to a very large family, who no doubt needed her to be strong.

As much as it seems that she managed this by looking at just the data before us, as she took her children back to the place she would have known the most, growing up in Hythe and having her own family nearby, we can naturally wonder if this moment took its toll on her.

Our modern minds today will probably know that bottling up emotions, may not always be the best solution to events as they may affect health and lives later on.

Was Amelia depressed either publicly or privately in later life?

It is a suggestion that at very least, going by what she had to cope with and do due to the sudden death of her husband, with also having a large family at the time and the fact that depression seems to have run in the family, this suggestion could be a reasonable one.

However, it must also be said that perhaps Amelia was not depressed, not being able to know the personality of the woman after so many years have past between her and us, we are unable to know for sure.

If she wasn't depressed enough to let it affect her, could we then wonder if this was where Charles Henry got his strong headedness from, as we will see later on in this book?

...

On the 1861 census, we find Charles Henry, now a seventeen-year-old young man, living with his mother in Chapel Street in Hythe.

He was also a working man, being a painter[437], an income we can presume was very much needed in the Cutbush family at the time.

With Henry Cutbush, Charles Henry's older brother, not living with the family, at this time, this meant Charles Henry was the oldest boy/man in the family.

Could we imagine that maybe he tried to take the pressure away from his mother?

Did he carry a little bit of the stresses of having a large family, himself, at the young age of seventeen?

---

437 1861 Census.

If that was the case, did he end up having much of a childhood?

However, asking that, we could also question if indeed any Victorian child have much of a childhood?

Charles Henry Cutbush
– The Police and Family Man

Six years of living in the Kent seaside town of Hythe, being painter, perhaps wasn't quite to Charles Henry's liking. Perhaps it was all too quiet for him, he was after all a twenty three year old man now and maybe he was in search of an adventure that was different to all he had known before.

Either which way, Charles Henry took a train to London.

The train would have taken him just over two hours to complete and in those hours, he would have seen the Kentish countryside, the fields that may have reminded him of his early childhood and possibly his own father working on them, change to become busier, more populated and different from everything he would have known.

However, he had idea in his head, he wanted to join the Metropolitan Police force, a decision that certainly changed his life and in turn the reason we are researching him today.

He joined A Division (Westminster) on 2nd December 1867[438] and was given the warrant number of 49037.

1867, would also be an important year to him because of a personal circumstance that was, we can imagine, was possibly the actual real reason why he had taken that train journey and joined the police force in the first place, so that he could have a steady job. Charles Henry had married.

---

[438] Service File.

Charles Henry Cutbush married Ann Dowle on the 6th October 1867 in the church of St Mary the Virgin in Dover, Kent.

Ann was baptised on the 13th October 1843 in the Parish Church of New Romney in Kent[439], being the daughter of William and Jan Dowle. In 1851 the Dowle family were all living in the High Street of New Romney[440].

Charles Henry may well have needed a steady job, not only because he had married Ann Dowle but because at the time of their marriage, Ann was seven months pregnant.

…

The author felt she should visit St Mary the Virgin Church in Dover, as it is one of the buildings that we now know Charles Henry would have seen and been in, which is still there, for us researchers to see today.

Visiting this church, brought home to the author that Charles Henry's marriage to Ann Dowle was now not just a date within his lifetime, a fact to be mentioned in a book.

Instead, seeing the church that Charles Henry walked into on that October day in 1867, aged only twenty three years old.

The church where Charles Henry was waiting for future pregnant wife to walk in after him, one hundred and fifty one years ago.

---

[439] Baptism Record.
[440] 1851 Census.

The church that would officially allow him to spend the rest of his life with the woman he had chosen and be the father to her children.

Seeing the church, where we can imagine Charles Henry having all these thoughts, positive thoughts of his future, truly made Charles Henry's wedding date actually something more than just a fact in a book.

It made it something more special somehow.

In actual fact the word 'special' seems to suit the church itself. The church was shockingly beautiful to the author, because it is surrounded by a modern town centre with all the known branded shops.

However, all of a sudden there the church is, there is the history, situated on an interesting angle. A beautiful graveyard surrounds it, with headstones, still visible, dating back to the 1700's, with picturesque trees framing the building, which adds something more, to the view of it.

The church is Grade II listed and is situated on what was a site of a Roman bath. It was mentioned in the Domesday Book and was a part of the Pilgrim journey to Canterbury Cathedral, much like the church in Hythe that Charles Henry would also have family connections to, as mentioned earlier in this book.

St Mary the Virgin Church in Dover, where Charles Henry Cutbush married his wife, Ann Dowle in 1867. ©Amanda Harvey Purse.

Author at St Mary the Virgin Church at Dover, Kent.

When Charles Henry and Ann got married inside, it would have looked slightly different than what we see today as to us, the church looks complete and as if it has always looked this way.

However, in the 19th century the church was being remodelled so that the church could be enlarged and have more windows.

Charles Henry and his future wife would not have seen the tower exactly how we see it today as that restored in 1897, the year after Charles Henry's passing and in the Second World War, some of the windows got smashed and destroyed, so they had to be replaced.

However, the eight bells that would have rang out for Charles Henry's wedding day would have been almost the same bells that ring out today, with the exception of the treble bell, as they were made by Samuel Knight in 1724[441].

…

Charles and Ann have their first born on 4th December 1867, they name her **Amelia Jane Cutbush** and they baptised her in Westminster[442].

Amelia never marries nor does she leave her parent's home, both parents of which pass away before her.

---

[441] St Mary's the Virgin Church – History.
[442] Baptism Record.

St Mary the Virgin Church in Dover, showing the bell tower. A part from one, the bells within this tower today would have been the same ones that rang out on Charles Henry's wedding day.

She later becomes a Lady Superintendent for the Inland Revenue Postal Branch at Somerset House.[443] The part of Somerset House that held the Inland Revenue was in the New Wing.

The New Wing was firstly designed as townhouses for the Admiralty's family by Sir James Pennethorne, it was completed in 1856. Then the building was used to combine the Stamp Office, Board of Taxes and the Board of Excise under one which they called Office of the Inland Revenue.

Amelia passes away on 14th January 1953 at St Francis Hospital, East Dulwich and leaves one hundred and five pounds to her younger brother Charley Stokes Cutbush, who at the time of her death was a rent collector[444].

It is interesting to note, that in between the dates of 1948 when St Francis Hospital was ran by the newly made NHS and 1966, when it became a part of the King's College Teaching Hospital Group, the hospital that Charles Henry's oldest child passes away in, was described as being a part of the South East Metropolitan Regional Hospital Board. This hospital was then described as holding five hundred and forty five beds for the 'Chronic Sick and mental observation'[445].

---

[443] 1911 Census.
[444] Probate Record
[445] St Francis Hospital – History.

The New Wing entrance to Somerset House. Amelia Cutbush, Charles Henry's daughter would have walked through these doors for many years of her life.

Considering, an event that happened with her father that will be mentioned later in this book, the high possibly of Amelia being at home at the time of this event, seeing it happen and now knowing she ended her days inside a hospital for 'mental observation', it is very sad to join the dots here.

Could we ask ourselves if we have discovered another clue that mental illness may have ran deeply within the family members we have mentioned?

Also, could we push this suggestion further and now knowing this information, is it possible to suggest that after Amelia sadly saw the event with her father happen, it was a trigger, (that may have laid dormant) for the reason she ended her days, where she did?

We have already mentioned members of Charles Henry's family having connections to mental illness and now we may have discovered that his daughter has suggested connections to it too.

With knowing this suggested information, can we then look into these connections as a good basis for what is to come later in this story?

Although we couldn't possibly hope to fully understand what was going on in the mind of anyone we are researching, so far back in time and although these suggestions are hard to question, perhaps we could at least say that we are a little closer to comprehending events in some small way, when the time comes to read of them later.

...

At the time of Amelia's birth, the family were living at Number 10 North Street in Westminster, which meant that Charles Henry was living and working all within the same area.

From this we could presume that he must have got to know the area of A Division quite well at this point in his life. Charles Henry was only a Police Constable for two years, when in 1869 he was promoted to Police Sergeant.[446]

In 1871 Charles Henry and his wife have another child, another girl, who they named **Ellen Cutbush**. This name changes throughout the years as she later becomes known as Helen Cutbush.[447]

Born at home on 23rd January 1871 and recorded as 'Ellen Cutbush'[448], Charles Henry and Ann do not baptise her until eleven years later, when she is baptised in group with her brothers and sisters.

In 1881, when the family had already moved into Number 36 St Paul's Road, 'Ellen' was recorded as being at school[449]. She later becomes a book keeper[450], staying with her brothers and sisters until at least 1946[451].

She passes away in September 1957 at Surrey Mid-Eastern[452] at the age of eighty five.

---

[446] Police Service File.
[447] 1891 Census.
[448] Birth Certificate.
[449] 1881 Census.
[450] 1911 Census.
[451] Electoral Records.
[452] Death Record.

There was a suggestion that Ellen/Helen passed away in, what was termed, a mental hospital. This suggestion needed to be researched to see if it could be proved either way, so the author looked into the matter.

With deeper research, beginning with her death certificate, it has been proved that Ellen or Helen as she is stated on her death certificate, ended her days at an address that was West Park Mental Hospital.

West Park Mental Hospital was never actually called 'an asylum' because at the time it was being built, in the 1920's, the term 'asylum' was being fazed out and the term really became no more under the Mental Treatment Act of 1930.

Designed by William C Clifford, who worked as an architect for the London County Council, designing not just West Park Hospital but other hospital such as St Ebba's and Manor.

Work started on West Park in 1906 and it was mostly completed by 1917, however the council put a hold on the build so that money could be freed up to help the war effort. This meant that the official opening did not happen until 1921.

Once opened, West Park could hold two thousand patients and consisted on many rooms, such as a laundry room, plant rooms, kitchens, sewing rooms and even a ballroom.

Outside the main block, it had a water tower, a mortuary, chapel and the staffing block.

The hospital was beginning to have less and less patients by 1995 and by 2003, it was closed and suffered from an arson attack by the September of that same year, destroying some of the records[453].

Seven years later, most of the hospital grounds was knocked down and redeveloped into flats, that are worth nearly £500,000 today[454].

…

Ellen/Helen Cutbush passes away at West Park Hospital on the 4th September 1957, she was aged eighty five years old and on her death certificate it states that she passed away because of 'Cardiovascular Degeneration', which could mean a number of different things, such as Coronary Heart Disease. The death certificate also tells us that she was cremated[455].

Again, here we see another family member close to Charles Henry, being in a place for the unwell.

The author admits that writing about these family members ending their days in places such as these, is not an easy thing for her to do, because these are not just facts for her place before the reader, these were people, who had feelings.

However, at the same time, she didn't want to not tell the full story of a person. She does not judge any circumstance, in fact the author more times than not, tries her best to

---

[453] West Park Mental Hospital – History.
[454] Zoopla.co.uk.
[455] Death Certificate.

understand the people she researches, of what they must have gone through, putting herself in their shoes.

The reason for this is to hopefully allows the author to tell these stories in a more down to earth and real way, than just mentioning the facts, for the reader.

Of course, the author can never say that she completely understands the family members of which she researches, of what they may have felt within certain events to write it.

After all, how can she completely know?

However, this book is here because she wants to *try* to understand, she wants to see past the facts and see the human being behind them. Hopefully making them seem more real to the reader while doing so.

So, with Ellen/Helen, the author cannot help but feel sorry for her. Technically, this book's main character is Charles Henry Cutbush, so when his life does eventually end, it would be easy to think that this book should end there too.

However, how can it really?

We have just learned that his daughter, who actually was at home when her father passed away, who was actually in the same room as him when the moment happened, (which will be discussed in more detail later) ended her days inside a hospital for mental illness in 1957. A whole sixty one years after her father's passing.

This, and all the emotions this event must have brought to other members at the time, proves that any dated fact doesn't just end after an author writes of it.

By looking a little deeper into these people's lives we can discover so much more, rounded 'facts' to make these people, whole. Or at least we can try to, in any case.

We can never know what the actual thoughts that were happening inside Ellen/Helen's own head for all those years were, after seeing what she did, as mental illness can take on many different forms and can be very personal to the person living with it.

However, as much as we have used past generations of the Cutbush family to try to understand why an event happened for Charles Henry, they are also the same family members that were related to his daughters.

We can only imagine what this information might help to explain for Charles Henry's children as well as for himself.

...

With a wife and two children to pay for, we can imagine another promotion was welcomed by Charles Henry, this came in 1873.

However, to become Inspector of the Metropolitan Police force, Charles Henry had to walk away from the area he had known in A Division and be transferred to C Division[456].

It was around this time that Charles Henry was involved in the 'suppression of the notorious night houses of Panton

---

456 Police Service File.

Street and other adjacent streets'[457], with Superintendent J. H. Dunlop.

This was the police movement to completely remove businesses, where houses were been used as brothels. We will later see that Superintendent Dunlop meets with Charles Henry again for a presentation ceremony, later in this book also.

On 24th June 1875, another child was born to the Cutbush family, they name her **Winifred Cutbush**[458], again she doesn't get baptised until 1882 with her brother and sisters.

Winifred later marries Augustus Francis Lindsay Crawford in 1920 in Cardiff, Wales[459], Augustus was born to John (a coachman) and Louisa Crawford on the 9th June 1870 in Battersea, London[460], being baptised on the 8th October 1870 in All Saints Church in Newington[461].

Winifred was Augustus's second wife as he had married Annie Helen Rayfield (born in 1864[462]) on the 3rd September 1898 in St Michael's church in Lambeth[463] and they lived together in Croydon[464].

---

[457] Morning Post - 24th August 1891.
[458] Born Record.
[459] Baptism Record.
[460] Birth Record.
[461] Baptism Record.
[462] Birth Record.
[463] Marriage Record.
[464] 1911 Census.

Author across The Thames from a place Charles Henry would have known very well. Scotland Yard.

However, Annie passes away on 5th October 1919[465], a year before Augustus[466] remarries Winifred Cutbush. They have no children together and Winifred passes away on 12th December 1952 in Hendon, Middlesex[467].

…

A year later, Charles Henry gets transferred back to A Division but this time he was to be an Inspector of the area he knew[468].

The reason for this move was because of the Assistant Commissioner at the time, Colonel Labalmondiere had offered Charles Henry an appointment at the headquarters at Scotland Yard. Charles Henry had accepted this role of being the 'principal assistant to Superintendent Harris'. [469]

In 1878, Charles Henry and his wife have a fourth child, again it was another girl and they name her **Caroline Cutbush**[470]. They don't baptise her until four years later when she was baptised at the same time as her brother and sisters.

Caroline doesn't marry and continues to live with her parents until they pass on, when she lives with her sisters and brother[471] until she sadly passes away on the 9th

---

465 Death Record.
466 He passes away in 1936 in Hendon, London – Death Record.
467 Death Record.
468 Police Service File.
469 Morning Post - 24th August 1891.
470 Birth Record.
471 All Censuses.

October 1927 in Kings College Hospital at the age of forty nine years old[472].

Her probate states that she left two hundred twenty pounds, fifteen shillings and one pence to her younger brother Charley Stokes Cutbush.[473]

...

A year after the birth of Caroline Cutbush, Charles Henry gets promoted again to Chief Inspector in 1879[474]. This was due to the fact that Charles's superior, Chief Inspector William Harris had moved away from the Executive Branch at this point, becoming a Superintendent to S Division.

Sadly, William Harris was to only be a Superintendent for another ten years, when he passes away at his home at Number 28 Adelaide Road on Friday 15th February 1889[475].

He had been gravely ill since his duty in the 'Trafalgar Square disturbances'[476][477] when the bad weather of the day,

---

472 Death Record.
473 Probate Record.
474 Police Service File.
475 Hampstead and Highgate Express - 16th February 1889.
476 Hampstead and Highgate Express - 16th February 1889.
477 This was also known as the Bloody Sunday Riots of 1887.
Unemployment issues had been raging throughout the 1880's and in the summer of 1887, the people wanted to protest about not being listened to, understood and wanted to put their point across to the government. One such meeting of the people was being held at Trafalgar Square, against the order of the Metropolitan Police Commissioner, Sir Charles Warren, who feared trouble may arise if this meeting was to be allowed to happen. This meeting, on Sunday 13th November 1887, still went ahead, which caused a violent riot to happen between the police and the people.

took hold of him, of which he would not fully recover from.

He had to leave his post several times from that point on, until his death in 1889 and because of this illness, he was constantly on the sick list within the force.

However, he had always tried to return to work but on 25th January 1889, he was on duty, doing his rounds and visiting Hampstead Police Station, when he mentioned to Inspector Banks of that station, that he felt unwell again, taking to his bed on that Sunday of which he did not get up from[478].

His funeral took place at West Hampstead Cemetery, where,

'The body was met by the band and men of the S Division and also by contingents of officers and constables from other police divisions'[479].

It was also stated that,

'He was a man kindly and genial disposition, and was greatly respected by a large number of friends in Masonic and other circles, while in the division under his charge, he was held in the highest possible esteem by officers and men alike'[480].

Considering that Charles Henry worked with William Harris on a number of occasions, William Harris was at one-time Charles's superior and that Charles would have been by the time of William's death, a fellow brother Mason, we could then question if Charles Henry was one of

---

478 Hampstead and Highgate Express - 16th February 1889.
479 Kilburn Times - 22nd February 1889.
480 Hampstead and Highgate Express - 16th February 1889.

the crowd at William Harris's funeral at West Hampstead Cemetery on 19th February 1889?

Later, we will find out that our suggestion could be true with a little digging for more facts.

...

As the new decade dawned of 1880, the Cutbush's moved out of their home in Number 10 North Street in Westminster to the somewhat larger home of Number 36 Paul's Road in Highbury.

We know this because Charles Henry and Ann have another child on 23rd August 1880, which they name **Charles** (to be also known as Charley) **Stokes** (after Charles Henry's mother's maiden name, *a sign possibly of the closeness that was still there between mother and son*) **Cutbush** and on his birth certificate it states he was born at home at Number 36 Paul's Road[481].

The author has visited Number 36 Paul's Road because above all else, *it still exists.*

The author was quite surprised by the area because when you look at pictures of that address online, of course you see the beauty of the Victorian house but you do not get the sense of how busy this area is today, until you actually visit it for yourself.

At one end of the St Paul's Road is Highbury Corner, which is not only busy with heavy traffic but it is busy with human traffic. Especially, on a hot, sunny day when the

---

[481] Birth Certificate.

nearby and many public houses are full and the customers are spreading out to the street, like they were when the author visited the place.

When you pass those busy areas and the noise becomes like a bubble outlet, we do eventually come to the place in which Charles Henry Cutbush lived with his family, having been a policeman for thirteen years, so far.

The house towers above you as you look up at it from the street, there is two reasons for this. One is that you would be standing on a slight tilt heading downwards and the second is that there are seven, large, steps up to the, some would suggest *ironic,* 'Metropolitan Police' painted dark blue coloured door, that has an arched window above the door frame.

With the black iron railings surrounding the house, the stairway leading up to the door, plus the white large bricks coating half of the house and the rest of the house showing its sandy coloured smaller bricks, it was easy for the author to imagine this house being built in the same style as what was imagined to be the home of the fictional Victorian detective, Sherlock Holmes[482].

---

482 Written by Sir Arthur Conan Doyle.

Author at Number 36 St Paul's Road, one of the addresses Charles Henry lived in with his family.

One of the addresses Charles Henry Cutbush once lived with his family, while he was a policeman. ©Amanda Harvey Purse.

The windows were in the same arched design as the window above the door and the thoughts of the young Cutbush children looking out of these, perhaps waiting for their father to return home, after a busy day at work, could also be easily be imagined.

There was also a set of stairs going down and curving to the left of the main stairway. This can be easily imagined, to have once been the servants entrance to the servant quarters and kitchen, now today possibly an entrance to another flat.

...

A year later, in 1882 Charles Henry and Ann decide to baptise the children that haven't been baptised before, so on 2nd November 1882, Charley Stokes Cutbush, Caroline Cutbush, Winifred Cutbush and Ellen (Helen) Cutbush get taken to St Paul's Church to complete this task in Walworth, which was by Walworth Police Station[483].

The church is now called St Paul of Newington Church but when the Cutbush's would have known it, it was called St Paul of Walworth Church.

Built in 1856 by Mr. H Jarvis, sadly we, modern day researchers would not be able to see the church how Charles Henry and his wife would have done, when they took their children there, to be baptised.

This is because it was destroyed in World War Two. It was rebuilt on the same site, exactly one hundred years after it was first built, in 1956[484].

---

[483] Baptism Records from the church.
[484] St Paul of Newington – History.

...

Charley Stokes lives at his parent's address, even when his father had passed on, until 1901 when he lives at Number 182 Princes Road, Moss Side, Lancashire[485].

At this time, he was a Mercantile Clerk and four years later, on the 7th August 1905 he marries Jessie Margaret Green[486] in St Mary's Church in Horbury, Yorkshire[487].

It is easy for us researchers to see how these two people met, *for a change*, as Jessie was the landlady's of Number 182 Princes Road, niece.

The couple have their first child, a year after their marriage on 28th June 1906, they name her Winifred (possibly after Charley Stokes's sister) Margaret Cutbush[488]. Winifred was actually born in Dublin, Ireland[489] and by 1926 she was living at an address that will be known to us later on in this book, Number 3 Burnley Road, London.[490] Winifred later passes away on 7th April 1967 in Los Angeles, California[491].

The next child Charley and Jessie were to have, was Charles (possibly named after Charley's father as well as

---

[485] 1901 Census.
[486] She was twenty five when she married Charley Stokes Cutbush, being born on 18th October 1879. Her father was Arthur Robert Green, a wagon builder – Birth Record.
[487] Marriage Record.
[488] Birth Record.
[489] Birth Record.
[490] Electoral Record.
[491] Death Record.

himself) Arthur (possibly named after Jessie's father) Terence Cutbush.

He too was born in Dublin, Ireland on 29th December 1908[492] and when he grows up, Charles Junior seems to like travelling as on the 3rd September 1948, he travels from Liverpool to Egypt[493].

Considering the time in which he does this, when archaeology was at its height and possibly it's most fashionable, it is possible to suggest that this Cutbush may have had an interest in this subject.

He returns to England on the 25th October 1952[494], to then travel to Cape Town, South Africa, returning home on 15th September 1959[495], where he passes away in 1971 in Yorkshire[496].

...

The third child Charley Stokes and Jessie have was Alfred George Cutbush, born on 11th February 1911. The family were back in London at this point because Alfred was born in Stockwell, London[497], a place that a certain Number 3 Burnley Road was situated.

This is an address that becomes important later in the Cutbush story, however one look to the 1911 census shows

---

492 Birth Record.
493 Travel Records.
494 Travel Records.
495 Travel Records.
496 Death Record.
497 Birth Record.

us that this side of the Cutbush family wasn't actually living at Number 3 but rather Number 18 Burnley Road[498].

Alfred later marries Eleanor Avril Moore in 1932 in Wandsworth, London[499], she had been born on 29th November 1907, passing away on 26th April 1981 in Sidcup, Kent[500].

Alfred seems to have taken on his brother's taste for travel as he spends some time in St Lucia, arriving back to Preston on 5th March 1952[501]. Alfred passed away on the 6th March 1980 in Southwark, being buried in Greenwich on the 14th March 1980[502].

While Charley and his family were living at *Number 18 Burnley Road* in Stockwell, Charley was a Finance Manager[503], becoming a father again just two years later, on 14th August 1913, they named the child Albert Harry Cutbush, possibly named after Charley's younger brother[504].

In 1914, Charley and Jessie had to separate. Jessie lives with her children at Number 6 Lambert Road in London and the reason for their separation was because Charley had joined the army.

---

498 1911 Census.
499 Marriage Record.
500 Birth and Death Records.
501 Travel Records.
502 Death and Burial Records.
503 1911 Census.
504 Birth Record.

Number 18 Burnley Road, Stockwell. Where Charles Henry's son, Charles Stokes Cutbush lived. ©Amanda Harvey Purse.

Author at Number 18 Burnley Road, Stockwell.

He had joined the 3rd Line Deport as a Gunner on 7th August 1914, where he served for one year and one hundred and six days, being discharged with a good character but because 'his services were no longer required'[505], on 20th January 1916[506].

He was described as being thirty five and four months, five feet eight and half inches tall, his eyes were grey and his hair was dark[507].

At the end of the year when he came out of the army, Charley became a father again with Helen (possibly named after his sister) Kathleen Cutbush being born on the 20th December 1916[508].

A year later, in 1917, Charley re-joins the army, this time for the Royal Garrison Artillery, giving his last known address as Number 49 Aldebert Terrance, Lambeth[509] but by 1936 he was out of the army again and was living at Number 3 Burnley Road[510].

Jessie, his wife, passes away on the 20th September 1956, with Charley Stokes Cutbush passing away in the same year, on 8th November 1956 in Sidcup, being buried like his son Alfred, in Greenwich[511].

He left one thousand seven hundred and twenty one pounds, ten shillings and eleven pence to his daughter, who

---

505 Army Records.
506 Army Records.
507 Army Pension Records.
508 Birth Record.
509 Army Record.
510 Electoral Records.
511 Death and Burial Records.

by that time had married to become Helen Kathleen Young[512].

...

In the same year of Charley Stokes' birth, the Morning Post reports of Charles Henry being involved with the Police Orphanage Fete stating,

'The weather was unpropitious for the annual fete of the Metropolitan and City Police Orphanage at Crystal Palace yesterday. Nevertheless, the excellent object to be served attracted over 30,000 persons to Sydenham and extraordinary number taking the heavy showers of the morning into account...Mixing with the men of the force and friends were Chief Inspector Cutbush, executive branch, Scotland Yard.' [513]

Also at this point, one of duties Charles Henry had to deal with, was lost property. This was highlighted in the many reports in the newspapers, like this one written in the Daily Telegraph,

'Metropolitan Police Office, Scotland Yard. Found – about 10:45pm (11th) near Angel Islington, an open face Gold English lever watch. Engine – turned case bow and glass deficient – Application to be made to Chief Inspector Cutbush, Executive Branch, Great Scotland Yard'[514]

However, this was not the first advertisement of its kind that Charles Henry had to deal with, as this one written in London Evening Standard back in 1877, shows us when it states,

---

512 Probate Records.
513 Morning Post - 7th July 1882.
514 Daily Telegraph - 19th June 1882.

'Metropolitan Police Office – Found. On the 7th Inst at Craven – Hill, Bayswater a Bank of England Note – Application to be made to Chief Inspector Cutbush, Executive Branch, Scotland Yard'[515].

Charles Henry, did seem to not be completely happy in his role as Superintendent of the Executive Branch of the Metropolitan Police as he applies to be Chief Constable of Birmingham, around this time.

This was a role of which ninety other men went for and Charles Henry got down to the final five people[516]. However, this seems to be the only time, Charles Henry looks elsewhere for work.

...

Charles Henry and his wife Ann, have another child on the 1st December 1883, they named him **Albert Harry Cutbush.**

From the 25th June 1889, at the age of five Albert Harry, was in Stockwell College[517], which had opened in 1861 and would close in 1936[518].

Albert lives at Number 3 Burnley Road[519] until 1911, when he was living at Number 67 Everton Road, South Manchester[520].

---

515 London Evening Standard - 23rd August 1877.
516 Morning Post - 24th August 1891.
517 Admission Records.
518 Stockwell College – History.
519 Censuses.
520 1911 Census.

On the 11th March 1914, Albert becomes a Freemason by joining the Zetland Lodge Number 525 at Salford.

The Zetland Lodge was named after the Grand Master of the United Grand Lodge of England from 1844 to 1870, Thomas the Second Earl of Zetland[521], Albert had paid up to 1921[522].

Albert Harry, like his older brother before him joined the army, being a Gunner in the Royal Garrison Artillery, Registration Number of 114670 and on the 6th January 1920, he had received the Victory Medal[523].

Albert later marries Mary Gertrude Price[524] in September 1936 in Lambeth[525], she had been born on the Christmas Eve of 1913 in Wandsworth, London[526] and passes away on 30th June 2007 in Colchester, Essex[527].

They live together at Number 3 Burnley Road until Albert himself passes away on 21st August 1960[528].

He left his wife, Mary, the sum of four thousand one hundred and sixty four pounds, nineteen shillings and three pence[529].

---

521 Freemason – History.
522 Freemason Records.
523 Army Service Records.
524 After Albert passes away in 1960, Mary remarries three years later in December 1963 in Wandsworth – Marriage Record.
525 Marriage Record.
526 Birth Record.
527 Death Record.
528 Death Record.
529 Probate Record.

A year after Albert Harry Cutbush was born, his father, Charles Henry becomes a Freemason by joining the Strand Lodge Number 1987 in Covent Garden.

He joins on the 8th May 1884 and rather interestingly he states that his residence was 'Scotland Yard', *a sign perhaps that Charles Henry was spending more of his time there, than at home?*

We can easily imagine this to be the case, couldn't we?

He resigns from this lodge in 1895[530]. This is an interesting date as it was only a year before a major event in his life.

This does help us make possible suggestion if he knew that this 'major event' was going to happen soon?

Or was he feeling unwell at this point and felt he couldn't continue at the lodge?

In truth, we will probably never know but looking at this date with hindsight, however it is curious nevertheless.

---

[530] Freemason – History.

Cutbush
Or Cuthbert?

In true Cutbush style, myths surround Charles Henry in his career as well as in his family connections, where it can be easy to go down the wrong path. This time the confusion starts around 1886.

On the 23rd February 1886 a committee wrote a report into how the police conducted themselves within the 1886 riots between the socialists and the 'working man' in Trafalgar Square.

This was the occasion where five hundred and sixty three policemen of all ranks were held in reserve to help the sixty six policemen that were on duty on the 8th February 1886[531].

Events did not go well for the police; Chief Inspector Shore had reported to Colonel Pearson at Scotland Yard that a part of the rioting crowd were heading westward.

This meant, they were heading toward Oxford Street and to a small bunch of policemen that, according to London Evening Standard, was under the control of 'Inspector Cutbush'[532].

He was seen charging at the crowd several times with 'great energy' first, before contacting Scotland Yard himself at five pm stating there was a disorderly mob in Oxford Street and that assistance was needed[533].

---

531 Manchester Times - 27th February 1886.
532 London Evening Standard - 24th February 1886.
533 Manchester Times - 27th February 1886.

Although the report ended by stating that mistakes were made in the police, with miscommunication, not having enough men and calling in the mounted policemen[534], it at least seems as if the business men of the area were pleased with the police's support in this instance.

As in the courtyard of Marylebone Police Station it was suggested that Charles Henry was one of a few policemen that were presented with gifts from many of the tradesmen along Bond Street and Oxford Street as a thank you for the police services in the riots.

It was suggested that Charles Henry received 'a gold watch and chain of the valve of £25'[535].

...

A problem arises however, when newspapers other than the London Evening Standard, such as The Manchester Times describe the Inspector involved in the 1886 riots as 'Inspector Cuthbert'[536], it is also 'Inspector Cuthbert' who receives the gold watch and chain.

This can make us researchers think that the other newspapers have got the spelling of Charles Henry's name wrong, also when we find that 'Charles Henry Cutbush' doesn't hugely appear in the newspapers within his career.

Could this be because his name was being recorded as being 'Cuthbert' instead?

If so, what could this mean?

---

534 Manchester Times - 27th February 1886.
535 Globe - 1st April 1886.
536 Manchester Times - 27th February 1886.

Could we then look into the cases of 'Inspector Cuthbert' to find if there is another connection to Charles Henry's cases?

If we do a little more digging, we find, The Miss Cass Case of 1887, from which both names of Inspector Cutbush (in newspapers such as the London Daily and Herts and Cambs Reporter and Royston Crow to name a few) and Inspector Cuthbert (in newspapers such as Hampshire Advertiser) were being stated as doing the same things within the same case.

Could this then further the suggestion that the newspapers had made a mistake with the spelling of his name?

If so, can we use this spelling of 'Cuthbert' to fill in the gaps of Charles Henry's career?

...

On the Boxing Day of 1881 at nine pm the police at Edgware Road was informed that a man attempted to murder a girl at Number 1 Southwick Crescent, Hyde Park.

The address was a lodging house run by a Mrs Caroline Ferne and 'Inspector Cuthbert' immediately went to this address and found out a German, called Emil Fansolow had tried to murder Clara Annie Byford, aged eighteen and the housemaid of the lodging house, by shooting her with a 'five chambered revolver'[537].

---

[537] Taunton Courier and Western Advertiser - 28th December 1881

Emil had tried to kiss the housemaid, however when she had pushed him away, he shot at her twice. The first bullet missed and the second hit her in the left breast.

She ran away from him and managed to alert the owner of the lodging house. When the police arrived, Emil had tried to commit suicide by slitting his throat and shooting himself.

However, he was still very much alive to tell PC Granville, 'I did shoot the girl because I loved her'[538].

Inspector Cuthbert sent for Dr. Capon of Edgware Road in the absence of the division surgeon, who in turn sent both patients to St Mary's Hospital[539].

Out of all the stories that the newspapers report of 'Inspector Cuthbert', this one sounded the most poignant to Charles Henry's story, as we have already mentioned two cases within Charles Henry's family where there had sadly been, suicide connections.

It also has an importance when we consider that this could be suggested as being a moment that Charles Henry was actually seeing an attempted suicide with a gun, for himself. Something that hauntingly comes around again later on in this book.

Does this open up questions to what happens later?

Does this help to explain events that are not that far away?

---

538 Taunton Courier and Western Advertiser - 28th December 1881.
539 Taunton Courier and Western Advertiser - 28th December 1881.

Could we understand the event when it happens more now because of what we have just found out about a case that 'Charles Henry' had to deal with?

Sadly, no.

This is a case of us travelling down the wrong path, this was an example of how easy it is to get carried away with events that we may think have a connection to the person we are researching[540].

The author wanted to show this example because although it has brought us to a blocked wall, it might have been a route we might have taken, that anyone might have taken.

She didn't just want to show all the workings out of examples that eventually lead us somewhere positive, because quite often that's not what happens with research.

The author did find it odd that most of the cases involving the name Cuthbert, were within the Marylebone, Edgeware Road area.

However, when the newspapers of Diss Express dated the 5th March 1886, Abergavernny Chronicle, dated 5th March 1886 and London Daily News, dated 1st March 1886, showed something, the author thought that this *something* could be the possible answer to her odd feeling about the research.

...

---

[540] The author would like to point out that she had researched many cases involving 'Inspector Cuthbert', before her results showed they were not always mentioning Charles Henry Cutbush.

There was an Inspector James Cuthbert within the Metropolitan Police force at the time.

James Cuthbert was the Inspector of D Division, which puts him working in the area of Oxford Street and surrounding areas, *including Marylebone*.

James Cuthbert then. goes on to become a Superintendent of K Division by 1902[541] and was Superintendent of X Division by 1905[542].

Now, we have to tread carefully with this information.

It is now quite possible that Charles Henry was not sent to the lodging house in Hyde Park, he might not have seen the attempted suicide of Emil.

However, what does this mean about the other cases we have mentioned?

With the Miss Cass case, quite a few newspapers actually spell Cutbush with one (as far as the author has found to date) newspaper spelling it Cuthbert.

This can make us feel fairly sure that Charles Henry Cutbush was involved in the investigation of the Miss Cass case and for that reason this case will be mentioned later in this book.

However, the author would also like to point out that this is now debatable, because the Miss Cass case starts within the

---

541 Kilburn Times - 31st January 1902.
542 Willesden Chronicle - 28th April 1905.

area of Oxford Street/Regent Street area, an area of which we now know Inspector Cuthbert to have worked.

The riots of 1886 is also an interesting one, newspaper reports both name the different surnames fairly equally, but the report on the Inspector receiving a gold watch and chain for his actions within the riots have (as far as author has found to date) always has been stated as 'Inspector Cuthbert'.

Also, the Marylebone Police Station from which we now know Inspector James Cuthbert worked his cases from, the suicide case being one of them, was just a few streets away from Oxford Street, where the rioters went to.

So, we can now begin to question, was Charles Henry Cutbush's role, a physical part of the 1886 riots?

It is certainly debatable for the reasons already mentioned.

...

In 1887, Charles Henry Cutbush becomes a Superintendent for the Executive Branch of the Metropolitan Police force[543].

He describes his own role as working within the same building as the Chief Commissioner and Colonel Pearson and although the Telegram machine was not in his office, it was under his control so that he could communicate with all police stations.

---

543 Service File.

He also, had control of policemen that were sent on special duty, prepare police orders and in very special moments he had control of police movements without having to take orders from his superiors, Colonel Pearson or Sir Edmund Henderson[544].

Could this suggest if Charles Henry made any action at all, his actual involvement in the 1886 riots wasn't actually on the ground but away within the offices of Scotland Yard instead? It is a suggestion of a possible answer.

His Executive Branch role made him in charge of police spending, hence why he was in involved The Curtis Bennett Inquiry of 1888, which will be discussed in more detail later on[545].

He also, was involved in trying to get better pensions for the policemen, often almost working a trade unionist against the departments he worked with.

He had another role within the police force at this point, as he was also in charge of some lodging houses.

Lodging houses, were being put under the control of the police since the uproar that was caused because of the overall state of them and the bad living conditions tenants had to cope with.

Now every room of a lodging house was inspected by the police. A placard was placed inside each property, to let the owners know how many people should be lodging there at one time. This was decided by calculating the minimum

---

544 Parliamentary Report – 1886.
545 MEPO 7/50.

space needed for a person and measuring the space to be used in the lodging house.

Each bed should have fresh linen and proper ventilation and men and women should have separate spaces unless they are married.

Police under Division A, which was the closest to Charles Henry's area, *as he was working within Scotland Yard*, governed areas such as Artillery Row, Dacre Street, Great Peter Street, Great Smith Street, Old Pye Street, St Ann Street and Strutton Ground[546].

---

546 Dickens Dictionary of London 1888.

The Miss Cass Case

In the July of 1887, 'Charles Henry' was suggested as being involved in the Miss Cass case.

Miss Cass was born in 1864 in Stockport[547], she had moved to London to work for Mrs Mary Ann Bowman in her premises along Southampton Row, working as a Seamstress.

She had been working for Mrs Bowman for three weeks, when on the night of the 20th June 1887, *the night of Queen Victoria's Golden Jubilee*, she, Mrs Bowman and Mrs Bowman's niece decided they would go out to watch the street celebrations.

Somehow, the ladies managed to separate themselves from each other and Miss Cass ended up near Regent Street, walking towards All Saints, Langham Place.

Perhaps, not knowing her way around, she then turns back towards Regent Street, this was the area and the moment she meets up with PC Bowden Endacott, who arrested her and charged her with disorderly conduct.

PC Endacott later claimed that while watching her, he had seen her accost at least three different men, as she walked up and down the street.

He told her, that he had seen her do this several times in the last six weeks, of which she denied, eventually stating that although she had been in London for about six weeks, she had not ventured out at night before.

---

[547] Birth Record.

Nevertheless, Miss Case was taken to the local police station and after asking for Mrs Bowman to prove her innocence, she was bailed out by the same woman and later dismissed with a warning.

Mrs Bowman was not happy with just walking away from this situation because of how the police had treated Miss Cass, especially the way she had be classed as a prostitute when there was no evidence to state this.

She wrote many letters to people of importance, such as Sir Charles Warren, the Commissioner of the Metropolitan Police, to hold an inquiry into seeing if PC Endacott should have any form of punishment because of his behaviour.

This worked and an inquiry was made. Within the inquiry Sir Charles Warren wanted to know if the charge sheet within the local police station of which Miss Case was taken, had been endorsed by the magistrate as this would disprove the bad conduct of the policeman because this was what normally was done.

…

It was suggested that Charles Henry produced Mr. Newton's charge sheet and it was he who had stated that it had *not* been endorsed[548].

Mr. Abrahams, the legal assessor for Mrs. Bowman, jumped on this information by asking 'Charles Henry', if it was normal to have someone described as a prostitute on the charge sheet.

---

548 Hampshire Advertiser - 13th July 1887.

He replied that 'the constable had no right to describe the person unless he had knowledge that was a fact'[549], he carried on by stating,

'That in South London, the custom was to accept the evidence of one constable as hundreds of persons have been convicted on such evidence.'[550]

However, like we have already discussed, although the majority of the newspapers quote 'Inspector Cutbush' in this matter, there are still some newspapers, already mentioned, that quote 'Inspector Cuthbert'.

Also, when we consider the area in which Miss Cass was picked up and taken to the local police station and that we are in the same area in the same time as where Inspector James Cuthbert worked, could this suggest that Charles Henry's involvement within this case, is now also debatable?

...

In the October of 1887, Charles Henry was presented by the request of the subscribers of the Police Guardian 'a handsome purse containing 50 sovereigns' by Chief Superintendent Dunlop[551].

A high sum indeed and perhaps showing how well-liked Charles Henry actually was within certain areas of his workplace, for the subscribers of the Police Guardian newspaper to suggest such a thing should happen to him.

---

549 Hampshire Advertiser - 13th July 1887.
550 Hampshire Advertiser - 13th July 1887.
551 The Police Guardian - 21st October 1887.

There is a possible suggestion that Charles Henry does not forget this moment, as we will see in a letter later on.

The Curtis Bennett Inquiry

We now turn to almost exactly a year later, when in July 1888, Charles Henry was involved in The Curtis Bennett Inquiry, *almost by his own doing.*

We know this was certainly Charles Henry this time as we still have Home Office letters we can see today, some letters were written to Charles Henry, some written about Charles Henry and some written by Charles Henry, himself. Which is quite amazingly, that letters of the person we are centralizing our research on, can still be read today.

The author wanted to mention this case, not just because Charles Henry was involved in it but that through it we may get to know a slight side to this man we have been researching through this case.

We may get to see a part of his personality at a time, when his connections to the Ripper case, had not formed yet. When he was three years away from retiring and eight years away from a dramatic event.

Probably to the dislike of the police force, the newspapers were quite quick to pick up on this inquiry stating,

'For sometime past a secret inquiry has been proceeding at the Home Office before Mr. Curtis Bennett, the Westminster magistrate, into the conduct of certain officials at Scotland Yard which promises to rival in the public interest the revelations at the Board of Work inquiry'[552].

---

552 Reynold's Newspaper - 15th July 1888.

This probably put added pressure on the police to get, not only an outcome in this inquiry, but an outcome that would feel correct to the public and the press.

'The affair has hitherto been kept a profound secret. Charges have been brought against the officers of having received bribes in connection with clothing and building contracts. The whole of the Police Accounts is under scrutiny and the evidence elicited has, it is stated, already justified the holding of the inquiry'[553]

When looking at these two newspaper articles on the starting of the inquiry, the word 'secret' appears.

This might suggest to the public and perhaps us researchers, even now, that the police were not keeping everyone in the know, as if they were hiding this inquiry from anyone.

This can in turn make us instantly unsure of the information we are being told.

This could be another example of an event involving the policeman we are researching, where the actions seem to be, at first, suspicious.

Was he a man that always knew more than he let on?

If we believe this here, with this case, could we then believe Charles Henry knew more than he let on in a future case of the Jack the Ripper murders?

The author is not trying to state that this was indeed the case. Or even that these are suggestions the author has thought of.

---

[553] The Star Newspaper - 15th July 1888.

However, the author wanted to show an example of how interesting it is that sometimes a single word can lead us to thinking all sorts things and makes us question actions later.

The author would again like to play fair with this by questioning how 'secret' this inquiry could actually have been, if the newspapers were already writing of it?

Also, when we consider that the newspapers also knew when the inquiry had ended and by that time knew what it was about?

As The Star newspaper indicates when stating,

'The Scotland Yard Inquiry, to which we referred to the other day is, we understand has now finished. It seems that someone in the Receiver's Department had been suspected of taking bribes or commissions from contractors.'[554]

...

However, let us start at the beginning. This case starts with a Mr. Harry King Evans, he was an accounting clerk in the Office of the Receiver for the Metropolitan Police force.

He came to Sir Charles Warren's notice at the time because the Commissioner thought someone was leaking information to the press and although Mr Evans was receiving a wage of five hundred pounds, it was known that he was in debt to the sum of three thousand seven hundred pounds.

---

554 The Star - 16th July 1888.

This information was known because the debtors had actually contacted Sir Charles Warren, themselves, because they had issued a summons on Mr. Evans' workplace, which initially was the police force, to try to get their money back.

This information must have laid in the back of the Commissioner's mind while he hired Wonter and Co, private investigators, to investigate who might be selling news to the newspaper.

He may even have highlighted his suspicious feeling of Mr. Evans in this matter because of knowing of his debt problems.

Sir Charles Warren's feeling made it so that, the investigation targeted mainly on Mr. Evans and although no evidence was found to suggest it was Mr. Evans that leaked any details to the press, the investigation did unearth another problem.

It had seemed at first, that Mr. Evans had lent money to the sum of thirty pounds in 1882, to a company called Newton and Cook, a company that had a police contract for brushes and sponges[555].

However, later information showed it was actually the other way around, the company had actually lent Mr. Evans money instead.

Although this company had written off the debt, this sprang up questions of why they had wipe the debt clean and the

---

[555] Working from Number 3 and 5 Wardour Street, Soho – Post Office Directory 1888.

Home Secretary was not happy with the news of Mr. Evans' insolvency, so demanded his resignation in the June of 1887.

The Home Secretary was also fast on finding a replacement for Mr. Evans, as a correspondence within the Home Office shows us by stating,

'Vacancy in Receiver's Office caused by the resignation of Mr. H. K. Evans – Recommends appointment of Mr. A. E. Hall to vacancy.' [556]

This caused even more problems for Mr. Evans as at the time he had tried to solve his debts by agreeing to pay one third of his salary to his debtors but now the Home Secretary had taken his salary away from him, as a Home Office letter shows us by stating,

'I am directed by the Secretary of State to inform you that he agrees as to the adoption of proposal contained in your letter of the 17th ult, for the assignment of one third of his salary and one half of any future salary he may receive for the benefit of Mr Evans creditors.'[557]

...

Mr. Evans' superior at the Receiver's Office wanted to clear Mr. Evans' name so spoke to Sir Charles Warren and asked him for an inquiry, this is where Curtis Bennett comes in as he resides over this eventual inquiry.

---

[556] Home Office Register Correspondence - 22nd June 1888.
[557] HO151/4 - 8th February 1888.

There was also the issue of Mr. Evans' pension, of how much he would be paid once leaving the force, as a Home Office letter shows us when stating,

'With reference to the application for a pension from Mr. Evans, a clerk in your office, I am directed to inform you that he has requested Dr. Gover, Medical Inspector of the Prisons, to examine this gentleman with a view to further the medical certificate.'[558]

Mr. Evans does eventually get his pension, as a letter from the Home Office to the Receiver's Office shows us by stating,

'With reference to former correspondence I am directed by Mr. Secretary Matthews to inform you that he has now been pleased to grant a superannuation Allowance of £195, 6, 9 per annum to Mr. H. K. Evans.' [559]

Meanwhile, former Detective Sergeant Charles Butcher of C Division wrote to Charles Henry, stating that he had completed some private detecting work for Mr. Evans, costing thirty pounds and he had not been paid.

Charles Henry sent this letter to Sir Charles Warren without replying to the detective, Sir Charles then sent the letter to the Home Secretary.

It is this letter that seems to be the reason Charles Henry was drawn into the inquiry firstly and his behaviour in the matter, highlighted him further, as a Home Office letter to Sir Charles Warren states,

'I am to call to your attention to Mr. Bennett's remarks respecting the conduct of Superintendent Cutbush and to say that Mr.

---

[558] HO65/61 - 14th July 1888.
[559] Home Office letter to the Receiver's Office - 31st July 1888.

Matthews would wish you to obtain from that officer and forward to the Home Office any observations that he may think fit to offer'. [560]

...

Charles Henry does as he was told and writes a response to his behaviour. This is an interesting document for so many reasons.

Firstly, it is of the hand of the policeman we are researching.

How lucky are we researchers to have anything of the person we are researching, for his handwriting that has been stored away within files, for us to still see today?

A document that he had touched, a document he had taken time over to communicate with and for us to hear his own words as we read the document to ourselves.

Secondly, this can show us, that he may not have always liked the orders in which he was given. For example, the feeling in this letter can seem to pick out a certain undertone of dislike in it.

However, Charles Henry still completes the orders, *in his own manner of course*, but he still completes them.

Thirdly, can this document allow us to get to know Charles Henry any more than what we have done already?

Well, let us see as we hear what he writes,

---

[560] Home Office letter - 14th July 1888.

'I beg to state that I am quite unconscious of doing or saying anything that could be construed into disrespect, or to any want of respect to Mr Bennett.'[561]

In this statement it could be suggested to be taken in two ways, he either generally seems in shock that someone had taken his actions in a hurtful way or it was the start of a backhanded apology.

He continues by stating what he thought had happened,

'I was examined by Mr. Bennett, Mr. Pennefather and Mr. Evans and it is probable that when the latter insinuated in his opening question that I had been instructed by the Commissioner as to what evidence I should give, that I replied somewhat sharply; and possibly I did so to other questions put to him as he seemed to assume that I was there as a hostile witness.'[562]

Here, it could be suggested that Charles Henry was trying to claim his innocence while also admitting that he realises his manner was sharp.

One wonders if Charles Henry had known he could be quite sharp in his manner at times. Was he always 'hostile' when asked questions?

Was this because he thought he should never be questioned for his actions or did he honestly believe he was just good at his job and should be left to do it? These are all good suggestions to think about as we read on.

---

[561] Letter from Charles Henry Cutbush to the Home Office - 21st July 1888.
[562] Letter from Charles Henry Cutbush to the Home Office - 21st July 1888.

One wonders if Charles Henry had a meaningful side to him, or whether this next statement was another backhanded sentence as he also writes,

'I can only express my very deep regret that anything I should have said, when questioned by Mr. Evans, should have caused Mr. Bennett to think I was guilty of want of respect to him, and to assure him that I am quite innocent of any such intention.'[563]

He carries on trying to explain why he behaved the way that he has, possibly highlighting that although he was apologetic, he still believed his actions were fair, when he writes,

'With reference to the candour of my statement, the remark is probably based on a question, as to who, in the Receiver's Department, I had ever heard speak of Mr. Evans. I requested permission to decline answering this question; but on the Receiver's pressing Mr. Bennett to force it, I replied. It appeared to me to be an attempt on the part of Mr. Evans to endeavour to implicate any person he possibly could, who had at one time gossiped about him, or his businesses'[564]

Was Charles Henry right to think this of Mr. Evans or did Charles Henry have his own agenda by hinting this about Mr. Evans?

Was Charles Henry acute to how someone was, by watching their actions or was Charles Henry a man that like to seemed polite on the surface but there was always a slight dig at a person in almost a revengeful way, underneath?

---

[563] Letter from Charles Henry Cutbush to the Home Office - 21st July 1888.
[564] Letter from Charles Henry Cutbush to the Home Office - 21st July 1888.

Two suggested different possibles taken from reading a paragraph of a policeman's own words, either one could be right, either one could be wrong.

...

Charles Henry then, tries to defend himself which of course can seem the natural thing to do, but can it also suggest that Charles Henry was confident man to do so?

When we also consider, that this whole circumstance may have caused Charles Henry to lose his job, he at this point, had no idea on how this was going to go for him.

Could this further the idea that he confident or perhaps he blind slighted to think he could not have possibly lost his job?

He could have been extremely apologetic, maybe slightly putting his point across but instead he feels he needs to explain his side of the story or how he felt when he was being questioned, when he writes,

'I was from the first treated as though I attended there as an enemy of Mr. Evans, and I submit that reference to my examination will show that this is so. I felt this, and I certainly answered with dire (Sic) regard to caution; but to the best of my recollection I answered every question explicitly'. [565]

Charles Henry ends the letter by, in a sense, advertising himself.

---

[565] Letter from Charles Henry Cutbush to the Home Office - 21st[h] July 1888.

He writes of how many years he had been in the police force and yet he had never been questioned before, he even hints of how well liked he was in not just the force but with the public themselves, when he states,

'I have been upwards of twenty years in the police force, and have never yet been censured. On the contrary I have been commended by Magistrates, the Secretary of State, the Commissioner and the public with whom I have had to deal.' [566]

...

However, if Charles Henry thought that his letter would put an end to this issue, he would be mistaken as Mr. Bennett replies,

'I have perused the copy of an explanation by Mr. Cutbush in reference to remarks I deemed it necessary to write in regard to his manner and evidence before me when sitting at the request of Mr. Secretary Matthews at the Home Office, and I am bound to state that the same is entirely inconsistent with the facts' [567]

This response was written just six days after the letter from Charles Henry was written and signed, so the speed in which Curtis Bennett writes could be taken as being quite telling.

Was he eager to hear what Charles Henry had to say?

Was he expecting Charles Henry's response to be in this tone and he was ready for him?

---

[566] Letter from Charles Henry Cutbush to the Home Office - 21s July 1888.
[567] Letter from Curtis Bennett - 27th July 1888.

If this is so, does this mean that Charles Henry had become predictable?

Was his behaviour always of this tone or at the very least, most of the time?

Another suggestion to add to this is, did Curtis Bennett know of which buttons to press to get a reaction from Charles Henry?

If this is a possible, who could have told him and why?

These are only suggestions of what we can question when looking at documents from thinking outside the box. Mr. Bennett carries on by explaining how he took the event, by stating,

'Immediately on his entering the room in which I held the inquiry, I asked him to take a chair. His answer was as follows, given in an insolent and defiant manner, 'Before I sit down or answer any questions, I wish to be informed what my position is here.' I informed him that this inquiry was held by me at the request of the Home Secretary, he then sat down but from the first to last his evidence was given in a most unbecoming manner and after one or two formal questions by me, he in answer to a question by me and not the Receiver of the police or Mr. Evans, said he declined to answer the question... At the conclusion of his examination on leaving the room, he slammed the door with such force as to shake the whole room...'[568]

This describes a very different picture of what happened and in truth the only people who would have known what actually happened were the four men in that room.

---
[568] Letter from Curtis Bennett - 27th July 1888.

However, we have got to ask ourselves what did Curtis Bennett have to gain for stating Charles Henry behaviour in this matter?

He didn't have to mention his behaviour at all in the report as he was tasked to do another job and yet he still does. Was Charles Henry's behaviour really that shocking, that odd even, to mention it?

It does seem so from looking at this from the outside, after so many years on. What did Charles Henry have to gain by stating it did not happen the way in which Curtis Bennett had mentioned it?

Was he simply trying to save his job, his reputation?

If we do take the event through the eyes of Curtis Bennett, did Charles Henry really think he was not going to be picked up on this?

Did he really not forward think enough to see that his behaviour would be called into question?

Surely, to be a Superintendent of the Executive Branch of the Metropolitan Police meant that Charles Henry had some intelligence, so could he really not see what was going to happen once he slammed that door?

...

If we stay with the slamming of the door action, it would be easy to say that this proves Charles Henry had an angry personality, but this is also one moment in time, that happened to have been recorded.

It may not necessarily mean he was angry all the time and the question of why was Charles Henry angry at that point, surely needs to be pondered on, if only for a second or two.

In looking for an answer to this, perhaps a letter written to Henry Matthews, the Home Secretary might suggest a possible answer when it states,

'Mr. Evans it would appear had given offence to the Executive Department some time back by his criticisms on returns from the Department relating to estimates, especially to Inspector Harris who had filled the post now by Superintendent Cutbush. Mr. Cutbush is the Superintendent of the Executive Branch and amongst other duties, he manages the Newspaper Department. Cutbush states that he knows no one who has any feeling against Mr. Evans'. [569]

Mr. Evans it seems, had a history with the Executive Branch of the police force. He had criticised the whole department, including its head at the time, Inspector Harris previously.

For Charles Henry to also have been mentioned within this letter and for him to be quoted, must suggest that Charles Henry was fully aware of the situation and what Mr. Evans had criticised.

However, instead of Charles Henry fighting worded fire with worded fire, instead of Charles Henry getting angry towards Mr. Evans this time, like we may have expected if only going on Curtis Bennett's view, he was simply quoted as saying he *'knows no one who has any feeling against Mr. Evans'*.

---

[569] Letter to Home Secretary - 12th July 1888.

This statement must include himself and it was only written nine days before Charles had to write his response to the way he behaved in the inquiry, what changed in that time?

We will possibly never know, however now knowing some of the pass history between the Receiver's Office and the Executive Branch in the police force, it certainly can show a different picture to what we may have been thinking before and can prove that *nothing is always as it first seems*.

...

This last letter also helps us with something else, for the first time mentioned in this book, we now have evidence of yet another role Charles Henry had within the police force, for he *'manages the Newspaper Department'*.

At first, it may seem that Charles Henry did not win this battle as another letter from the Home Office to the Commissioner states,

'With reference to the report from the Superintendent forwarded by you on the 23rd instant respecting the evidence given by him before Mr. Curtis Bennett, I am directed by the Secretary of State to transmit here with a copy of a further letter on the subject from Mr. Bennett and to request that Superintendent Cutbush may be severely reprimanded.' [570]

This was done and Curtis Bennett was let known of it by the 1st August 1888 as a letter from the Home Office to him states,

---

[570] Letter from the Home Office to the Commissioner - 31st July 1888.

'I am to inform you that the officer in question has been severely reprimanded.' [571]

However, this was done at a time when Charles Henry was on leave[572], so this action does have a slight feeling that it was done to quieten Curtis Bennett, perhaps even Mr. Evans too and it was done when Charles Henry was out of the way.

The author also wonders how severely was his reprimand if he doesn't seem to have lost anything, i.e. pay, fine or role and he wasn't even there are the time?

However, Charles Henry being on leave might have also been seen as the form of punishment, while also managing to keep the main character of this growing saga out of the way.

Another possible reason for Charles Henry's absence could be due to illness, we know later on that some of the newspapers that report on Charles Henry's retirement also quote that Charles Henry had been ill for some time.

For example, the Globe states,

'He has been failing health for some time past, caused partly by the many changes since the resignation of Sir E. Henderson, 5 years ago'. [573]

---

571 Letter from the Home Office to Curtis Bennett - 1st August 1888.
572 Service Record.
573 The Globe - 22nd August 1891.

This would place the start of his illness in 1886, two years before the Curtis Bennett Inquiry and two years before the Jack the Ripper investigation.

Also, for a newspaper to mention his illness and we will see later that the Globe newspaper was not the only paper to state this, could we presume it was a well-known thing?

Was this why Charles Henry was really on leave?

Although we may not know the answer to these questions, they do make us think about the man himself and whereas we might have just thought of Charles Henry being 'ill' some time later.

Perhaps we can now think of his illness starting earlier and if this was so, how it must have been for not only himself but his close loved ones to be around him, who were possibly unable to help him…

The Start
Of Jack the Ripper?

Charles Henry was certainly back in his office, six days after the Home Office had written to Curtis Bennett stating that Charles Henry had been reprimanded.

We know this because two reports that were headed for the Commissioner's desk, found their way to Charles Henry's desk first and he in turn added his name to them.

These reports seem to be written by Inspector Edmund Reid of H Division, the same Edmund Reid we had mentioned earlier in this book with another side of the Cutbush family tree.

Inspector Edmund Reid had only just become Inspector of H Division the year before, being transferred from J Division and he had probably already seen how depressing the area in which he now governed could be with the sad death of a new born baby girl in Skidmore Street, Mile End[574].

However, that case was not all that Edmund had to deal with, there was a murder that has been suggested being the start of a serial killer's spree and a murder whose details often float in the backs of people's minds when discussing the Martha Tabram murder, of which Charles Henry eventually adds his name to the reports of.

---

574 This was the case of Florence Lovett being accused of murdering her new born baby while she was in the house on her own. She sister had found the baby in a cupboard covered in blood, however it later turned out to be that the child had died at birth. - Inspector Reid: The Real Ripper Street by Amanda Harvey Purse.

This was the murder that had happened in the April of 1888 and Inspector Reid was at the inquest of. The murder of Emma Elizabeth Smith.

Emma Smith

Emma Smith had been living at Number 18 George Street and this was the address she left at six pm on the 3rd April 1888, the Easter Bank Holiday.

She was next seen at quarter past twelve on the 4th April, being in the company of a man described as wearing dark clothes with a white scarf.

However, just four hours later, Emma had managed to get herself back home at Number 18 George Street.

She had been attacked in Brick Lane, her face was covered in blood, her ear had been cut but the fatal inquiry was the instrument that had been thrust up inside her.

She was taken to the local hospital, where she was able to given a description of her attackers to the police that were at her bed, before she died.

Inspector Edmund John James Reid. Whose reports of the Martha Tabram murder, Charles Henry read and wrote his name to.

Her attackers were never caught, although in later years the murder of Emma Smith has been suggested as being a 'Jack the Ripper' killing.[575]

In addition, on the 25th June 1888, Inspector Reid also had to investigate the attempted murder of Annie Patterson and her brother, John Barry, at her home at Number 18 Grove Street[576].

These are just a few examples of how the year of 1888 was turning out to be a busy one for not just the Inspector but the whole police force within he and Charles Henry Cutbush belonged.

Martha Tabram

Inspector Reid was then given the details of another murder within his area by Inspector Ellisdon on the 7th August, this would be the murder of which Inspector Reid writes his two reports on and *Charles Henry comes into contact with*.

On the 6th August 1888, a married woman who had separated from her husband and the father to her children, was out drinking with a suggested friend called Mary Ann Connelly within the area of Whitechapel Road.

---

575 Inspector Reid: The Real Ripper Street by Amanda Harvey Purse.
576 Annie's husband Richard Patterson had stabbed John Barry in the jaw with a knife and had turned his attention to his wife by cutting her four times, once on the finger, twice on the face and once on the arm. The police were called and when Inspector Reid arrived at the house, he described the address as being like a 'slaughter house'. Richard had made his escape while the brother and sister were taken to the local hospital – for more information please see Inspector Reid: The Real Ripper Street by Amanda Harvey Purse.

Her name was Martha Tabram, although because she had been living with another man, a Mr. William Henry Turner, an occasional hawker and carpenter at the time, she was also known as Martha Turner.

Almost three months before her death, she had turned thirty nine years old and life had not been easy for her in those thirty nine years.

She had seen her parents separate and pass on, she had married, taken on her husband's child that wasn't her own, had her own children by him.

She had then separated from her own husband and had been in and out of the Workhouses.

Now it seemed she was drinking heavily with Mary Ann Connelly; the drinks being paid by a Private and Corporal.

She leaves the last public house that she visited along Whitechapel High Street at around eleven forty five pm, however she was apparently not alone.

Martha goes with the Private to an alleyway that runs alongside the White Hart public house called George Yard, while Mary Ann Connelly goes along to the next alleyway, called Angel Alley, with the Corporal.

Although Mary apparently leaves the alleyway soon after without hearing anything, Martha, it could be suggested[577], would not be that lucky.

---

[577] As Martha was found some time after this, we cannot be sure if Martha had left George Yard, only to return later.

Five hours later, Martha was found on the landing of George Yard Buildings, within George Yard.

She had stabbed as many times as years she had been alive, thirty nine times, with apparently two different weapons, one dagger and one bayonet.

The first policeman upon the scene was PC Barrett, who also claimed to have seen a Private at roughly the same time as the suggested murder.

With this being stated, Inspector Reid took PC Barrett to the Tower of London, where a parade of men was set up for hopefully the PC to identify the person he saw that night.

However, he was unable to[578] as was Mary Ann Connelly when she was eventually brought in to do the same. Inspector Reid appeared at Martha's inquest and afterwards wrote his report of the murder.

Inspector Reid's Martha Tabram reports which was recorded under MEPO 312/3 and 312/5[579], also seem to have Charles Henry's signature on them.

---

578 For more information please see Inspector Reid: The Real Ripper Street by Amanda Harvey Purse.
579 National Archives.

Author outside The White Hart public house. Showing the archway to what would have been George Yard and the scene where Martha passed away (above).

The mortuary photograph of Martha Tabram (left).

It can be seen in a 'Summary of Contents', that seem to be originally dated on the same date as Inspector Reid's reports of the same murder[580].

Could this lead to the suggestion of a certain chain of events?

Such as Inspector Reid wrote his reports. He sent them to Alexander Carmichael Bruce, the Assistant Commissioner of the Criminal Investigation Department's office.

However, this office was also in the same place as Charles Henry's office and perhaps before they got to the Assistant Commissioner, the reports happened to fall on the desk of Charles Henry.

Charles Henry then read them and after adding his 'Summary' to the reports with his signature, he then sends them on to Assistant Commissioner?[581]

This is of course only a suggestion that stands with reasonable possibility but is still open to debate.

Just above his signature on the reports was stated,

'3rd Special Report.
Submitted in accordance with P.O, 9th February 1888. The body has been identified by Henry Tabram of 6 River Terrace, East Greenwich, as that of his wife, but she left him some years ago, and has recently been regarded as a prostitute. The witnesses have attended both the Tower and Wellington Barracks and two men have been identified at each place, but all have been able to give a

---

580 Dated 16.8.88 and 24.8.88.
581 MEPO 321/3 and 312/5.

satisfactory account of themselves on the night of the murder. Enquires are being continued.'[582]

And,

'5th Special Report.
Submitted in accordance with P.O 9th February 1888. The inquest was resumed 23rd, inst. When the evidence was completed, and verdict of wilful murder against some or persons unknown returned. Enquiries are being continued.'[583]

...

In the September of 1888, a letter was printed in the Pall Mall Gazette which mentions Charles Henry.

We do not know who wrote this letter as it is signed 'Not an Outsider' rather than a name, but with looking at the material mentioned, the overall feel and the fact that one of Charles Henry's roles was within the Newspaper Department of the Police force, could we suggest it may have been written by *Charles Henry himself*?

It starts,

'Sir – I was much astonished to read in tonight's issues your comments on the resignation of Mr. Monro in the cause of which you intimate that Sir C. Warren will probably find himself in difficulties thereby. Had the services of either of the other Assistant Commissioners been lost, there might have been some cause for the remark'.[584]

---

582 MEPO 321/3 and 312/5.
583 MEPO 321/3 and 312/5.
584 Pall Mall Gazette - 3rd September 1888.

The boldness of this statement is interesting and can possibly show the reason why the writer does not put their name at the bottom of this letter.

However, perhaps we are also seeing the true nature of the writer here, maybe the writer has a natural bold personality?

Also, it shows the writer's dislike for Mr. James Monro, a prominent figure in the Jack the Ripper investigation.

'How Sir C. Warren can find himself in a difficulty with such exceptional and capable men as Colonel Pearson and Mr. Bruce to support him, I cannot see – It is impossible for an outsider to know the immense valve of their services to the force – the one with his long military service at his back, the other with his keen perpetration and profound legal knowledge.' [585]

This can show the author doesn't just know of Colonel Pearson and 'Mr. Bruce' but also knows of their backgrounds too and gives the suggestion that the author quite likes them.

Does this suggest the writer also likes authority as well?

'Then too, you have the quite overlooked Superintendent Cutbush, who seizing the opportunity at Sir Charles Warren's accession has stood at the helm ever since, safely guiding the good ship, the 'Metropolitan Police force, through the stormy water of 1886-8 or change the metaphor he, the veteran in the service hassled the child Commissioner over the rough road of his own choosing'.[586]

This paragraph could actually show us a lot about the writer.

---

585 Pall Mall Gazette - 3rd September 1888.
586 Pall Mall Gazette - 3rd September 1888.

If this letter wasn't written by Charles Henry, it sure seems as if the writer likes him very much and if the letter *was* written by Charles Henry, he certainly seems to like to toot his own horn.

The writer of this letter was basically stating that although Charles Henry was often overlooked, he had actually done so much for the police force.

In addition, the writer wanted it known that in fact it was down to Charles Henry that the police force made it through the 'stormy waters' because if people did not know it then, he was at the police force's helm.

This certainly gives us a different look to Charles Henry and just shows what this book is trying to do, as every human has different traits to make us more rounded and this is a good example of a different trait.

It could also be suggested that this trait carries on, when the writer states,

'The only surprise of 'those in the know' is that Mr. Cutbush has not received the vacant Commissionership; certainly no one would have filled the post with greater distinction than he. Perhaps however, there is better fortune in store for him. Uriah Heep found it his best policy to be 'humble', Mr Cutbush finds the opposite course the most suitable to him and succeeds equally well'. [587]

Was Charles Henry expecting to be Commissioner instead of Sir Charles Warren?

---

587 Pall Mall Gazette - 3rd September 1888.

Did other people presume Charles Henry to be the next Commissioner?

This concept may not seem a strange one if we look at Charles Henry as a policeman, after all he had a policeman for many years, he had been given many promotions and he was a policeman of high rank.

However, Charles Henry was not just a policeman, was he?

As we have seen he was born in the market town of Ashford. Seeing his father work the fields in a florist family business, he had also moved to the small seaside town of Hythe, where he was a painter.

However now, Charles Henry was being suggested as a person that could have become Commissioner of the Metropolitan Police force in London.

Stated like this, it does seem to make this feat ever more amazing for the main character in this book.

James Monro. A player within the Jack the Ripper investigation. Did Charles Henry not get on with this man, within his working career?

Sir Charles Warren, who became the Commissioner of the Metropolitan Police force. Another player with the Jack the Ripper investigation. Did he take on a role that Charles Henry's wanted?

The Beginning
Of the End?

At the same time as this letter, Charles Henry was also being mentioned as taking his normal role within Police Orphanage Fund as a handicapper[588].

This action of helping the fund was to continue, as seven months later, on the 22nd March 1889 Charles Henry was at the Adelphi Theatre helping to make the matinee of various entertainments held for the Police Orphanage Fund, 'a great success'[589].

This was also the same year that a person Charles Henry used to work with died, we already have mentioned a suggestion that Charles Henry was one in the crowd of people that went to Inspector Harris's funeral.

We can find out now, when we look a little deeper in to it, that the Hampstead and Highgate Express newspaper list him as being there in their article about the funeral,[590] as well as Superintendent Foster of the City Police.[591]

---

[588] Hampstead and Highgate Express - 18th March 1888.
[589] London and Provincial Entr'acte - 16th March 1889.
[590] Hampstead and Highgate Express - 23rd February 1889.
[591] For more information on the lives of Superintendent Foster and the City policeman that were involved in the investigation of the murder of Catherine Eddowes, a suggested Ripper victim, please see Jack and Old Jewry: The City of London Policemen who Hunted the Ripper by Amanda Harvey Purse.

Chief Superintendent Alfred Foster of the City of London Police. Another player within the Jack the Ripper investigation, who was at Inspector Harris's funeral with Charles Henry Cutbush.

CHIEF SUPT. FOSTER.

Foster's grave at the City of London Cemetery. He passes away just a year after Charles Henry. ©Amanda Harvey Purse.

We can never know how events might have affected the people we are researching, especially this far back in time.

However, we have already discussed that Charles Henry was known to be 'unwell' from 1886, now by 1889, he had also been involved in an inquiry where he could have lost his job.

Is it possible that the likely hood of him possibly coming close to losing his role, came as a surprise to him?

Could he have thought of his role within the police force as being safe and secure and now this inquiry made him questioned his 'safely blanket'?

In addition, he had now also lost the man he had taken over his police role from. For Charles Henry to be listed as one of the people there at the Inspector's funeral, must mean that Charles Henry liked or indeed cared for Inspector Harris and now he had now passed away.

Can we wonder if the passing of this person did not help Charles Henry's state of mind?

With so much time that has passed, we will probably never know for sure but that is not the point of this book.

It is not the point to just mention the facts but to think around them, to think what they could mean if we allow our minds the freedom to come up with questions because *of the facts.*

Knowing that a question can never be wrong but may let us think more about the man behind his policeman role, the man behind the name of 'Charles Henry Cutbush', for us to perhaps catch a glimpse of the human being that he was.

Six months after the funeral of Inspector Harris, Charles Henry was one of the officials for the Metropolitan Police Swimming Club for A Division and in the May of 1891 Charles Henry helped to appoint Mr. William George Morant[592] as the new Head Constable for Reigate and Red Hill with his testimonial[593].

Charles Henry's retirement wasn't that far away however, that being also in 1891 and we may wonder now that if Charles Henry's illness was known back in 1886, why did he waited until 1891 to retire?

...

There could be a number of factors here, firstly although it might have been well known that Charles Henry was 'ill' by other people but it might not have become apparent to him at that time.

Secondly, if he had left in 1886, it would have meant he had worked only nineteen years in the police force.

He would have known, through the years of fighting for a better pension as mentioned earlier in this book, that nineteen years would not guarantee a good pension.

While leaving in 1891, he would have worked twenty four, almost hitting the twenty five year mark, which would have given him a better pension.

---

592 He was the Chief Inspector and Assistant Head Constable of Reading at the time.
593 Sussex Agricultural Express - 16th May 1891.

In addition, something happens to Charles Henry in the July of 1891, the Birmingham Daily Post states,

'Mr Charles H. Cutbush, who for so many years, has been the Superintendent of the Executive Branch at Scotland Yard is seriously ill. It is feared he will never be able to resume his duties'.[594]

It is never explained what has happened and to date the author is still searching for that answer, but it cannot be denied that whatever it was, it was bad. The words 'seriously ill' shows us how bad this event was.

This coupled with the fact that in his pension records it states that he had 'knife wounds to his right thigh', not caused while on duty,[595] it does seem suggest something was not at all right with Charles Henry.

Of course, there is also the possibly that those 'knife wounds' could have occurred at any time and may not have happen in the July of 1891, however sadly facts do not seem to sit comfortably for Charles Henry's state of mind, at this point.

Another reason for his retirement in 1891 may have been because he wanted to wait to see if the Act of 1890 for better policemen conditions, would be passed.

In the June of 1890, a meeting of all the Superintendents was held in Charles Henry's office in Scotland Yard to discuss the better pay interview that was answered by the Inspectors and constables within force, would meant that a

---

[594]Birmingham Daily Post - 30th July 1891.
[595]MEPO 21/21.

new Superannuation Bill, which was championed by James Monro, would later be passed[596].

We know this was passed as the Gravesend Reporter, North Kent and South Essex Advertiser stated,

'There is little doubt that the severe strain of his duties, coupled with his energetic endeavours to obtain for the police the benefits which they now enjoy under the Act of 1890 has been the primary cause of the state of health which has made his retirement desirable'. [597]

...

Charles Henry retires on the 11th August 1891, getting paid to the 10th and starting his pension the day after, the amount was two hundred twenty one pounds per annum, this was signed away by Acting Superintendent, Mr. W. Davis[598].

He was described as being forty seven years old. Five feet nine inches, his hair was brown with his eyes being hazel. His complexion was fair and he had a 'particular mark, defect or infirmary by which he may identified: Knife wounds, right thigh'.[599]

This description will be even more interesting when we read of an event at the end of this book.

The newspapers caught hold of the retirement of Charles Henry and once again they mention his failing health by using the words 'for some time past', but while also

---

[596] The Times – 18th June 1890.
[597] Gravesend Reporter, North Kent and South Essex Advertiser - 5th September 1891.
[598] Pension Records MEPO 21/21 File Number 10282.
[599] Pension Records MEPO 21/21 File Number 10282.

describing Charles Henry as 'one of the best-known heads of police'.

It also stated that he was 'commended by the Secretary of State for services rendered under the direction of Superintendent J.H. Dunlop in connection with the total suppression of the notorious night houses in Panton Street and other adjacent streets'.

It finally ends with stating that Charles had 'several testimonials have been presented to him during his service in the force'.[600]

---

[600] Morning Post - 24th August 1891.

Location
To set a scene

In the April of that same year, the Cutbush family were living at Number 3 Burnley Road, Stockwell so because of this, the author visited both Number 3 and Number 18 Burnley Road.

Number 18 is also important to this research of the Cutbush family, because it was at this address that Charles Henry's son, Charlie Stokes, lived in as mentioned earlier in this book.

The author wanted to visit this place for two reasons, firstly because of its importance to Charles Henry, as a way of paying her last respects to the man she felt she had learn so much more about now, through this research of him and his family.

Also, this address was the last place in which Charles Henry lived, he was to never move again. So, the author did not just want to see the actual place where he lived but also get a feel for the area Charles Henry would have known too, *if that was still possible*.

The walk from Stockwell Underground Station to Burnley Road was a short one, but the author was a little worried that at first everything looked newer than what Charles Henry would have seen.

That was until she got half way down Stockwell Road and the houses began to start to look in the right, Victorian era.

With the houses on the right-hand side looking very much like Charles Henry's previous address at St Paul's Road as mentioned earlier in this book, but without the steep stairs leading up to the main door.

When the author took a turn to the right she was already in Burnley Road and instantly the author felt at ease, as both sides of this slightly smaller street to Stockwell Road, were full of Victorian houses.

It wasn't long before the author was outside Number 3 and it looked very well maintained with a flat roof and sand coloured bricks that went down half way and white coloured large bricks completing the rest of the building.

Very much like Charles Henry's last address, there was a white painted stairway leading up to the main door and a set of stairs going down to what would have been the servant's quarters.

Amazingly, there is a way to see inside this address, today.

This is because Number 3 Burnley Road has been separated into three flats and in 2013 the ground floor flat, where Charles Henry's kitchen would have been and where his daughter, Amelia, was said to have been when a future event happened within this house, was on sale.

 You can still see the photographs of that one bedroom flat online with a floor plan. In 2013 it was suggested that this flat was worth £305,000[601].

The second floor was also on sale in 2015, so the photographs and floor plan of this can be seen too.

601Rightmove.co.uk.

This is perhaps more important to the life story of Charles Henry as this would have been where Charles Henry's study would have been. We will see soon how important his study was in a future event and in 2015 the now second floor flat was suggested to be worth £432,000[602].

...

Further along the same road but on the opposite side to Number 3, is Number 18 Burnley Road, where Charles Henry's son once had lived.

Number 18 today, stands out to passers-by for two reasons. Firstly, because instead of having the sand coloured bricks showing, it has a dark red coating over the building and secondly, it has a blue plaque.

...

---

[602]Rightmove.co.uk.

Number 3 Burnley Road, Stockwell. Charles Henry Cutbush's last ever address. ©Amanda Harvey Purse.

Author at Number 3 Burnley Road. As the author looked up at the doorway Charles Henry would have walked through, she couldn't help but think there was perhaps something missing from the building, *a blue plaque perhaps?*

The blue plaque was because Violette Szabo had also lived at that address at one time.

Born on 26th February 1921 in Paris, her family moved to London where she was separated from her parents to live for a short time in Northern France with her aunt during the Great Depression.

Afterwards, she was back with her family in London, going to a school in Brixton, where she learned English before working in a Woolworths in Oxford Street.

When the Second World War broke she was working at Le Bon Marche in Brixton[603], before she, joined the Women's Land Army.

She first worked in the fields of Fareham in Hampshire and then working in an Armaments Factory in Acton before enlisting for the Auxiliary Territorial Service, who sent her to Leicester for training.

Once her training was passed she was then set to work in places such as Shropshire, Anglesey and Frodsham.

However, after the death of husband, who was killed in the Second Battle of El Alamein, she became a British Special Operations Executive[604].

She was sent on two missions undercover in France, until she was captured by German troops just outside Salon-La-Tour.

---

603 Violette Szabo: The Life I Have by Susan Ottaway 2003.
604 Violette Szabo: The Life I Have by Susan Ottaway 2003.

She was brought in front of the Gestapo with her true identity now known and she was finally taken to Ravensbuck where she was shot in the back of the head.

She was only twenty three years old[605].

---

605 Violette Szabo: The Life I Have by Susan Ottaway 2003.

Charles Henry Cutbush
– His Passing

Sadly, if Charles Henry ever thought he would have a long retirement after the police force, this would not be the case.

Throughout this book, we have seen family members of the Cutbush family that have connections to suicide, some of these members Charles Henry could have possibly known in his early childhood, some members Charles Henry could possibly have not known.

We have also seen him losing his father and siblings at an early age, seeing death at an early stage meant he had to grow up fast.

He had the pressure of looking after a large family before he even had one of his own and he must have felt that he had always looked after his mother as she had lived with him until his death.

However, at the same time, this could suggest a person that may have still heavily relied on his last surviving parent.

We have also discussed events within his life, that may have been triggers towards an 'unsound mind'. Events that may not have first seem to affect him but events that stuck with him in the back of his mind, in doing this we have hoped to understand Charles Henry's final moments.

Moments of which was stated at the beginning of this book, that sadly Charles Henry has become more known for than his life and the people within it.

Mental illness is something we are still trying to understand today, so can we truly imagine what is must have been like for the person suffering with it, let alone the people surrounding that person, in the Victorian period?

The author has tried her best to put herself in the shoes of Charles Henry throughout this book, to find the best way to convey why his ending was what it was.

However, the author fully realises that she cannot truly know what was going on in his head when he took that final moment because everyone is different, everyone reacts differently to events but she hopes she has done something agreeable, even something peaceful for Charles Henry Cutbush within this book.

The author has hoped to make him more than just his death, more than a person that might have been related to a Jack the Ripper suspect.

Charles Henry Cutbush was a son, a father and sadly a man that had troubles in his head. Troubles he may not have understood himself but troubles that took hold of him and made him take his own life...

…

On the 5th March 1896, Charles Henry would have been fifty two years old for exactly two months.

He was at home and at two o'clock, in the afternoon, he was sitting in his study with his daughter Ellen (or Helen as we have seen was sometimes who she was quoted to be) on the first floor of the house.

His daughter was sitting in the corner of the room, reading, his other daughter was said to have been in the kitchen below, we do not know who, if any, other members of his family were at home at the time.

Ellen/Helen, at this time, looks over to her father and to her, he seemed strange in appearance but perhaps she was used to seeing this from her father by now, so she returns to her reading.

A moment later, a shot was suddenly heard in the room, we can imagine the bang of the shot was very loud, very sudden and echoed around the room and perhaps down to the kitchen underneath.

Ellen/Helen shockingly looks up from her book and sees that her father had taken out a 'pistol' that he had always carried in his pocket and had shot himself in the head[606].

...

We can only imagine what happened next, maybe deathly silence, maybe the house was full of shrieks and howls coming from his daughters.

Either which way, Charles Henry's doctor, Dr. White, was called from his address at Number 241 South Lambeth Road. A trip that would have roughly taken four minutes by horse and carriage at the most, or at least seven minutes by walking.

---

[606] Morning Post - 10th March 1896.

The author went to the doctor's address as it was not that far away from Charley Henry's home but in the opposite direction from Stockwell Underground Station.

The building is actually still there, which surprised the author a little to still see a Victorian building, untouched in the capital which is becoming more and more of a rarity.

The house, looked in the same style as Charles Henry's home, the same coloured sand brickwork and the white large bricks around the window and door frames and similar stairs leading to the front door, although it did look slightly smaller than Charles Henry's home.

Dr. White must have known his destination to his patient's home very well, when he was called to it on that Thursday afternoon again.
Not only did Dr. White later claim that,

'He had been attending Mr. Cutbush for insomnia and pains in the head' and that 'at times he had delusions, one being a rooted antipathy to Roman Catholics whom he believed were following him in order to bring him to ruin'.[607]

This suggested that he had been to Charles Henry's home on many occasions, but he would also later claim that he had actually visited Charles Henry on the morning of the 5th March 1896 and 'found him to be very excited'.[608]

One wonders if the doctor prescribed Charles Henry something to calm him, after all that would be the most natural thing for a doctor to do with a 'very excited' patient.

---

[607] Morning Post - 10th March 1896.
[608] Morning Post - 10th March 1896.

If this was the case, could we then wonder if this medication affected Charles Henry in some way?

Could this then explain why Charles Henry chose that day and in front of his own daughter to commit suicide?

More times than not, suicide can be a personal event for the person doing it and the author has always thought it was odd for Charles Henry to choose a time when he was in front of his own daughter to do it.

It seemed rushed, without thought, care or forward thinking. Something about this event jarred with the author, something did not seem right to her.

Could a new medication be the answer?

If Charles Henry had taken something within the late morning of that day, when the doctor first visited him, maybe it would have taken until the afternoon before it took on any kind of side effect.

With this questioned, could we then wonder if this was the reason why it had happened on that day?

Research into suicide also brings up the fact that some people take drugs such as muscle relaxants before... *acting*, as they want to feel calm, they don't want to back out from what they are going to do.

So, could this new medication to have calmed him, have helped Charles Henry do what he apparently wanted to do?

Of course, this is only a suggestion and just because suicide can be a personal thing for some, it may have never

Number 241 South Lambeth Road, Stockwell. The address that Dr. White, the doctor of Charles Henry Cutbush, lived. ©Amanda Harvey Purse.

Author at Dr. White's address. He travelled from this house to Charles Henry's home on the day, Charles Henry passed away.

occurred to Charles Henry what he was making his daughters see, after the event had taken place.

...

Not much has been written about this Dr. White, in fact he has only been mentioned by surname and his address at the at the time of Charles Henry's passing.

The author wanted to change this, to at least find out this doctor's first name at the very least so she began her research and she was actually able to find out more than she had first hoped that she would.

The research starts by looking into the history of Dr. White's address, Number 241 South Lambeth Road.

We find that the house was owned by a Mrs Mary A Höner in 1891, she was living there as a widower with her two daughters[609].

However, Mrs Höner sadly passes away in 1895[610] and the house was sold to Dr. White the year after, in 1896 when he appears on the electoral roll there with his wife[611].

It was extremely handy to find Dr. White on the electoral rolls as he doesn't seem to have stayed at Number 241 South Lambeth Road long enough for him and his wife to be mentioned on the census records there.

---

[609] 1891 Census.
[610] Death Record.
[611] Electoral Roll from 1896 – 1901.

In 1891, Mrs Höner owned the building and by 1901, Dr. White had passed his home business on to Dr. Benjamin Jones[612] and his family[613].

It is interesting to note that although Dr. Benjamin Jones appears on the 1901 census living at this address, in March, Dr White was still registering himself living at this same address on the 1901 electoral roll in August.

From this information we can see that Dr. White's first name and second name were *William Thomas* and from there we can find out that he was in 1829, the year the Metropolitan Police force, of which a future Charles Henry Cutbush would join, started.

He was born in London and by 1881 he had married[614] and was working as GP from his home at Belmont House, Southgate Road in Tottenham[615].

He stayed at this address for over twenty years when in 1896 he moved to 241 South Lambeth Road as already mentioned.

This statement is quite interesting because Dr. William Thomas White does seem to suggest that he had visited and cared for Charles Henry *for a while* in his quotes to the

---

[612] 1901 Census – Benjamin Jones was born in 1861 in Carmarthenshire. He would have been forty years of age when he moved in and took over Dr. White's business.

[613] Benjamin's wife Alice Jones, born 1861 in Scotland and their two sons David Bruce Jones, born 1892 and James Andrew Jones, born 1898. – 1901 Census.

[614] Susanna (sometimes written as Annie) White, born 1832 in Worcestershire – 1881 census.

[615] 1881 census.

newspapers at the time of Charles Henry's passing, as already mentioned.

However, this new information can now make we wonder for how long was Charles Henry actually his patient for?

We now know that Dr White had only moved into his new address, which was not that far away from Charles Henry, in the year of Charles Henry's passing.

Could it be possible that Charles Henry was a patient of Dr White's before the doctor's move into the same area?

If this was correct, it would have meant that Charles Henry or indeed the doctor was travelling a distance of over an hour to see each other, at a time when, as we discussed earlier, Charles Henry could have been possibly quite ill.

This does seem to be a little odd and can make us question if there was not a doctor living nearer to him at the time, that Charles Henry could have used instead?

If Dr. White had only been Charles Henry's doctor for a few months in the year of 1896, could we then bring up the question of new medication here again?

Would it have been possible for Dr White to know of any side effect, any new medication innocently given to Charles Henry might bring, if Charles Henry was a newer patient to him than what we had first thought?

All interesting questions that now bring themselves to us because of finding out a little more about Dr. White, than we did before.

...

Many newspapers mention his suicide, like the Ipswich Journal, who stated,

'Shot himself at his home at 3 Burnley Road, Stockwell, following years of headaches and insomnia where he attributed to a blow he had received some years before'. [616]

This statement can make us wonder if this blow to the head happened in 1886, when his 'illness' apparently started, in 1891 when something happened and it was feared he wouldn't be able to return to his duties as a policeman or some time else?

Also, the same newspaper states,

'He had retired early from the police owning to an 'affection of the brain'. [617]

This last statement can make us question if this 'affection' was widely known in the police, in his family or the public for the newspapers to mention it?

Was this always what was meant when records and documents we have already mentioned, state an 'illness' for Charles Henry?

...

It is not often mentioned what happened to Charles Henry after he had passed away, research seems to stop after the moment Charles Henry sadly shoots himself.

---

616 The Ipswich Journal - 14th March 1896.
617 The Ipswich Journal - 14th March 1896.

However just because the soul of person has left the world at a singular moment, it does not mean that it is the end of the story.

To complete our story of Charles Henry, we will continue with as much information that there is out there for us to follow to gather the full picture.

When Charles Henry died on the 5th March at his home in Burnley Road, his inquest was resided over by a coroner who worked from St Thomas's Hospital.

Does this information make it is possible to suggest a new image in our heads now, instead of his body staying in his study and for the story to end there, can we now imagine that his body was taken the short distance to St Thomas's Hospital, where the inquest was held four days later?[618]

If we run with this theory, could we then ask ourselves if it was possible, that Charles Henry's body was cremated there? It is only a suggestion but one worthy to think about.

The outcome of the inquest was 'Suicide. Injury to Brain from pistol bullet inflicted by himself whilst in a state of unsound mind. Shock.'[619]

Now, when we look at this inquest outcome, one thing may stand out to us, because words can be important, words can allow us to see something more and one word can stand out here, even if it first seems to be an 'off the cuff' statement.

---

[618] Charles Henry's death certificate.
[619] Charles Henry's death certificate.

However, we have met with 'off the cuff' statements before with Charles Henry as mentioned at the beginning of this book, so let us look at this one too.

The word here is 'shock', if we look at the rest of the outcome it isn't much different from the newspaper article descriptions of his death.

However, the word 'shock' can suggest that something suddenly happened or it could possibly have meant *medically* in a state of shock, which is different.

Medically in a state of shock is when a person has very low blood pressure or a very fast heart beat which may lead to a Cardiac Arrest.

Either one of these meanings is interesting and can tell us a little bit more of the event than if we had not mentioned the inquest at all.

What possibly happened suddenly to have made him shoot himself?

Or why possibly was his heart racing or his blood pressure had dropped at this point to have made him shoot himself?

To possibly answer these questions, could we then bring up the suggestion of new medication again here to answer this?

All intriguing questions that, if anything, has now appeared to us to, at least, ask.

'But then face to face'

Another interesting fact is that the Coroner who oversaw Charles Henry inquest was none other than George Percival Wyatt, whose name may not been instantly be recognisable but he was a part of some famous murder cases of the time.

Such as when the parts of a body that was found in the grounds of the new Scotland Yard was being investigated in the October of 1888 and at the height of the Ripper Murders, George was sent another parcel of bones.

A young boy by the name of Alfred Tomlinson was walking along Sumner Road on Thursday 18th October 1888.

This would have been a road that the young boy knew well as his employer, Charles Brown, who was a hairdresser worked from Number 92.

Alfred happened to glance to the side of the road and saw a parcel in the gutter, *curious*, the boy stopped to have better look at it.

He opened the parcel, possibly hoping to see something of value that he could use, when what he saw instead was bones of a human being.

He took the parcel to his employer, who eventually took it to Peckham Police Station that was along the High Street. The Division Surgeon, Dr. Philip George Phelps, a prominent name within the Jack the Ripper case, was called in to have a look at the bones. He thought that the bones were of a woman's arm and that they could have been possibly boiled at one point.

At the same time as the doctor being called in, so too was the Coroner's Office contacted and from there, James Woodman notified George Percival Wyatt, the then Deputy Coroner of the North-Eastern Division of Surrey of the discovery. The bones were later taken to Camberwell Mortuary.

George's feelings over this matter was very much the same as the doctor's, who thought the bones were a prank made by a medical student. A medical student who might have heard of the body parts that were found in the grounds of the New Scotland Yard and because of that, he did not think it was necessary to hold an inquest for the bones[620].

...

However, this was perhaps not the most famous crime George was involved in the case of, as he was actually quite heavily connected with the case of a Glasgow born murderer, Dr Thomas Neill Cream, later to be nicknamed The Lambeth Poisoner.

Born on the 27th May 1850, Thomas Neill Cream moved to Quebec in Canada by the age of four with his parents. From there he went to McGill University in Montreal where he gained his MDCM degree, focusing of the effects of Chloroform.

He married Flora Brooks in 1876, however she died one year later of Consumption, Thomas would later be blamed for her death.

---

[620] Lloyds Weekly – 21st October 1888 and Manchester Times - 27th October 1888.

By the late 1870's, he had a brief spell in London, ironically, working inside St Thomas Hospital, the hospital that George Wyatt worked his inquests from.

He then travelled to Edinburgh by 1878, becoming a physician and surgeon. A year later, he was back in Canada, when a woman that Thomas was meant to have had an affair with, Kate Gardener, was found dead in an alleyway behind Thomas's office. She had been pregnant at the time and had been poisoned by Chloroform. Thomas moved over the border to America soon after that.

In 1880, the death of Mary Anne Faulkner, highlighted Thomas to the police again but due to lack of evidence, Thomas was let go.

In the same year, Miss Stack who was a patient of Thomas's, died. This time, Thomas highlights himself by trying to blackmail the pharmacist involved, blaming him for the murder.

Then on the 14th April 1881, Daniel Stott passed away after Thomas was treating him for Epilepsy with Strychnine. The death was officially attributed to 'natural causes' but again Thomas highlights himself by writing to the coroner, blaming the pharmacist for the death.

This time Thomas gets arrested with the wife of Daniel Stott who apparently was having an affair with Thomas. She turned on Thomas, to escape prison herself so it was Thomas, alone, that was sentence to life in Joliet Prison.

In an odd, perhaps unsettling fact, on Daniel Stott's headstone the words 'poisoned by his wife and Dr Cream' appear.

Although Thomas was sentenced to life imprisonment, he was actually released from prison in the July of 1891 after his brother pleaded for leniency and some say he paid his way out, using money he had inherited from his father in 1887.

After being released, Thomas moved to England and started living at Number 103 Lambeth Palace Road.

On the 13th October 1891 Ellen Donworth, aged just nineteen, met with Thomas. He offered her a drink and later she died from Strychnine poisoning.

The coroner at her inquest was George Percival Wyatt, he also received a letter, although signed 'G. O'Brien, Detective' it was later believed to have been written by Thomas, himself.

In this letter Thomas claimed to have information on the murderer of Ellen Donworth and if the government were to pay him three hundred thousand pounds, he would tell this information.

Dr Thomas Neill Cream, who wrote to the same coroner who resided over Charles Henry's inquest.

George dismissed the letter, claiming that it must have been written by a person looking for fame.

George was also the coroner at the inquest of Alice Marsh and Emma Shrivell, two other victims of Thomas Neill Cream, who drank from a bottle of Guinness, given to them by Thomas and later died in agony.

Thomas was eventually hanged for his crimes at Newgate Prison on the 15th November 1892 and in an odd twist of fate, this case brings us back to Jack the Ripper because the hangman, who hanged Thomas, a Mr. Billington, claimed that just before his body fell, Thomas stated 'I am Jack the...'.

However, this is a suggested quote because Major *William*[621] Henry Smith of the City of London Police force, another prominent name within the Jack the Ripper case, was also meant to have been at the hanging event of Thomas Neill Cream too, but did not claim to have heard this extra piece of information.

---

[621] New research into Major Smith of the City of London Police, proves that 'Henry Smith' was actually born 'William Henry Smith' – For more information please see Jack and Old Jewry: The City of London Policemen who Hunted the Ripper by Amanda Harvey Purse.

A sketch of a hanging happening outside Newgate Prison (top) and photographs of how Newgate Prison looked like in the year of Charles Henry's passing, 1896 (bottom).

William Henry Smith, who becomes Commissioner of the City of London Police force, who was said to be at the hanging of Dr. Thomas Cream.

However of course, this maybe the case that he could not have claimed it because he simply may not have heard it, as hangmen are closer to the prisoners than the viewing public.

...

When George Percival Wyatt resided at the inquest of Charles Henry, this would not have been the first suicide he would have encountered.

Sadly, in the year of 1886, Catherine Mellows, aged only thirty three years old was found at Number 1 Hansler Road, Crystal Palace Road in East Dulwich with her throat cut.

It had seemed that a few days before her death, she was acting oddly and did not sleep very well.
Catherine had threatened to commit suicide many times to her husband, Thomas Joyne Mellows, so as sad as this occasion was, it was sadly not unexpected.

The jury returned the verdict of 'Suicide while temporarily deranged'[622].

Certainly not an easy case to hear and one can only wonder how George Wyatt felt when he had to hear of another case of suicide, when dealing with Charles Henry Cutbush.

George would have known the area and possibly the house of which Charles Henry Cutbush passed away in as he had been living just a fifteen minute walk away from him, for a number of years at Number 33 Wiltshire Road, Lambeth.

---

[622] The Times – 1st July 1886.

George had been living at this address with his two sisters, Florence and Julia and his mother Emily Jane Mayhew Wyatt[623]. Sadly, the building George would have called his home before his marriage, no longer exists and has been replaced by a 1970's or a 1980's style estate of flats.

George had married Mabel (sometimes written as May) Hetley Betts in 1895 and she was due to give birth to their only child, Richard, in the year after of 1896, the year of Charles Henry's passing and a new address was looked for.

The fact that George's son, Richard, was born at home at Number 66 Tulse Hill on the 11th April 1896[624], we can presume George was living at this address with his wife at the time of Charles Henry's passing, which was only a month before.

This address was a forty five minute walk away from Charles Henry's home in Burnley Road[625].

Sadly, much of Tulse Hill was bombed during the war and George's address as he would have known it, no longer exists[626].

However, to get an idea of what George's house would have looked like, as many of the houses were designed at the same time, we can still look towards Number 47 Tulse Hill.

---

[623] 1891 Census.
[624] Birth Certificate.
[625] 1901 Census.
[626] Survey of London Volume 26, Lambeth: Southern Area – London County Council.

Number 47 Tulse Hill, Lambeth. As George's address at Number 66 was bomb damaged, this house gives us an idea of the style of home, George Percival Wyatt lived in with his pregnant wife at the time he would have resided over Charles Henry's inquest.

...

In an odd way, George has a slight connection to Charles Henry, in the fact that Charles Henry was born on 5th January 1844 in Ashford, Kent[627] and passed away, in the area of Lambeth, London, according to his death certificate.

Meanwhile. George was born on 9th January 1851 in Lambeth London[628] and passed away in Ashford, Kent.

In actual fact George Percival Wyatt, was buried on 7th February 1924 in All Saints Church, Biddenden, Kent[629] with his wife, Mabel Hetley Wyatt[630], nee Betts (1872 - 1941[631]) and his son Richard George Percival Wyatt (1896 – 1962[632]).

This means he was buried in a church that is only an hour's walk away from Sissinghurst Castle, the place that once was Cranbrook Workhouse and as we have seen earlier in this book, housed and sadly was the burial ground to two members of Charles Henry's family.

It is also mean that he was buried, amazingly, only half an hour's drive from the place in which Charles Henry Cutbush was born.

...

---

[627] Birth Certificate.
[628] Birth Record.
[629] Church Records.
[630] They married in 1895, the year before Charles Henry's death, in Lambeth – Marriage Record.
[631] Birth and Death Records.
[632] Birth and Dead Records.

Although, technically, George Percival Wyatt has no family connection to Charles Henry, because he as we now know was a part of Charles Henry's inquest, the author felt she must include him in one of her many visits for this book, as she had done a similar action by visiting Charles Henry's doctor's address.

So, the author visited George's last resting place in Biddenden and amazingly he is one of a *few* people she has researched in her books, which has a headstone.

The headstone stands prominent in a stone, in a Celtic cross style, very similar to Herbert James Cutbush's headstone, mentioned earlier in this book, at Highgate Cemetery.

Written upon the headstone are these words,

'In loving Memory of George Percival Wyatt for 42 years HM Coroner for the counties of Surrey and London. Who died February 7th 1924, Aged 72.
'But then Face to Face'
Also of his wife Mabel Hetley, who died August 1st 1941. Aged 69 years and of their son Richard George Percival, BSC ENG London 1st Hons. Who died May 8th 1962, aged 66 years'.

The area where the George Percival Wyatt is buried at All Saints church in Biddenden, today. ©Amanda Harvey Purse.

The headstone of Wyatt family. George Percival Wyatt was the coroner that resided over the inquest of Charles Henry Cutbush. ©Amanda Harvey Purse.

Author at the grave of George Percival Wyatt at Biddenden, Kent.

Charles Henry's
Possible burial

Now we have to turn to the burial of Charles Henry and this is where it sadly gets even more of a depressing concept, as we researchers may have noticed before, the funeral and burial of Charles Henry was not known to be published in the papers.

This is probably because in 1896, suicide was still classed as a crime and although there was more sympathy of this event by this time than in the 16th Century, it still meant that the person should not ideally be buried on Holy Ground.

They were generally cremated and then scattered. They were not allowed a funeral which might be the reason why records do not seem to have anything of Charles Henry's burial to date.

However, there is a *slight* possibility that Charles Henry *was* buried in the churchyard closest to his last address.

If this was the case, the burial had to be done between nine pm and midnight, as it was still thought of as an embarrassing slur on the family name.

If this indeed happened, Charles Henry would still be buried without a marker to show his name or his presence in this world.

This could also explain why Charles Henry's funeral didn't seem to be mentioned in the newspapers, because of the time of night it had to be done.

It is also worth noting that according to the South London Advertiser, under the subtitle of 'Suicide at Stockwell', Charles Henry's inquest, was held on Monday 'night'[633].

This is an interesting concept when we are discussing the possibility of Charles Henry either having a night time burial or a night time scattering of his ashes, to know that he had a night time inquest.

With this information known, the author did take the time to visit St Michael's Church, Stockwell. This church is currently not being used as another more modern but nearer to Burnley Road is being used instead, that being the Church of St Andrew, which is being shared between the two parishes, to date.

However, St Michael's would have been the church the Cutbush's would have known and perhaps the whole family would have gone to on a Sunday morning.

We know that this church was built for them to visit it because in the church's history, it is recorded that a part of the church was being repaired in 1896, the year Charles Henry died.

This church is actually not that far away from Burnley Road if you head toward Stockwell Crescent, so the author is wondering whether Charles Henry's private night time burial could have been held there.

The author wanted to visit this church because of this possibility, she wanted to see the last place Charles Henry might have been in and she wanted to pay her last respects

---

[633] South London Advertiser – 14th March 1896.

to finally say goodbye to a man that had been the central role in her research for this book.

While she did so she'd hoped that he thinks that she has looked at his character and events within his life, from the good, the bad and the upsetting to produce Charles Henry Cutbush in a more full, rounded way than what we may have thought of him before.

This is because, after all, there is always a life before any death and the author hopes the reader will agree, the lives of all the Cutbush family members have been, very interesting to meet along the way.

...

The church is very Gothic in style which was the classic design when Mr. William Rogers drew the plans up for it in 1839.

At the cost of roughly £4,125 this church was eventually built in 1841. The spire is decorated with a ring of small pinnacles and it does seem to add to the overall look of the building, which seems to be stretching and reaching up to the skies[634].

At the time in which Charles Henry might have known it, it had two entrances, so that the servants of the households of the surrounding area would not walk in with their employers.

One of the quirkier facts of this church is that it is facing west, away from Jerusalem, as most churches face east.

---

634 The History – St Michael's Church website.

St Michael's Church, where Charles Henry may have had his night time burial or scattering of ashes. ©Amanda Harvey Purse.

Author at St Michael's Church, Stockwell. London.

The plaque on St Michael's Church explaining that its tower was replaced in 1896. ©Amanda Harvey Purse.

Author at the plaque of St Michael's Church, Stockwell. The author pointing to the year of 1896, the year of Charles Henry's passing.

This is because St Michael's was turned around in the 1880's, so it is said, to give the church more space inside.

However, there were myths attached to this building that the church had to change around, so that it changed where the altar was because of a *suicide* had happened in the west end of it[635].

How completely odd is that piece of information?

Here we are, as researchers, trying to learn the history of a building because they may have accepted Charles Henry's night time burial upon their grounds even though he had committed suicide and now we know it has its own myths attached to it, surrounding the way Charles Henry had chosen to pass away.

Does this make it even more likely, that the church would have allowed Charles Henry's burial to have happen?

Where and why do myths take form?

Did the myth within the church happen because it was working on the true facts of Charles Henry death and the story got a little confused along the way, like Chinese whispers?

A suggestion for us to think about as we come to the end of this story.

---

[635] The History – St Michael's Church website.

Charles Henry Cutbush's Family Tree

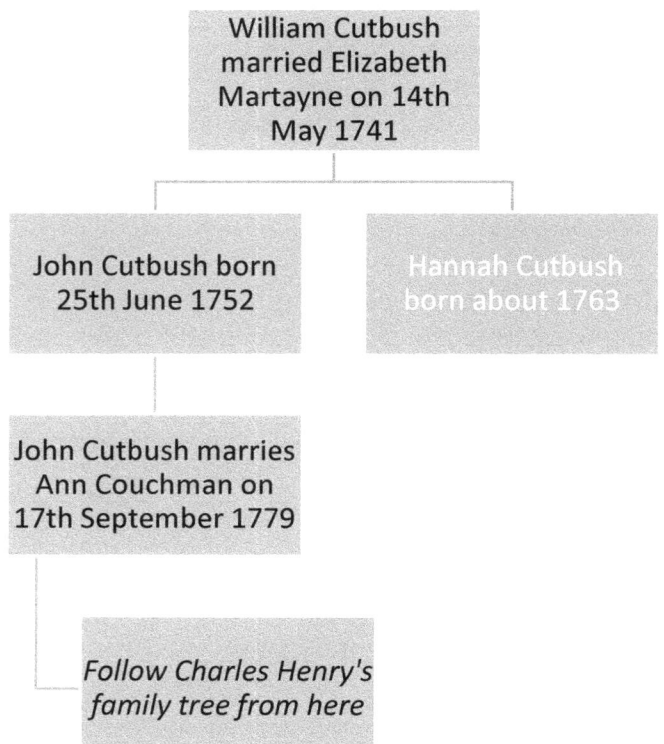

292

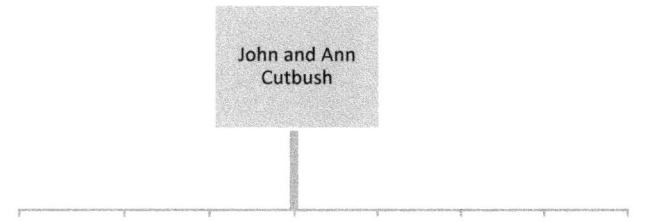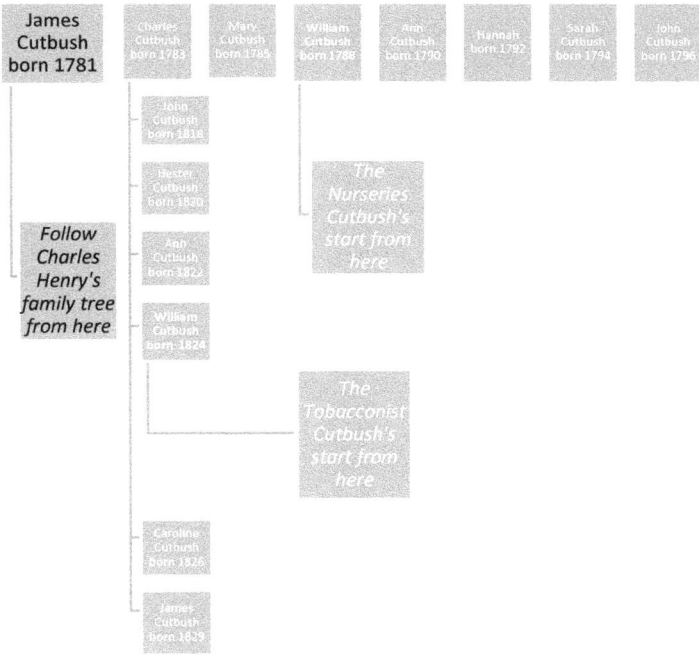

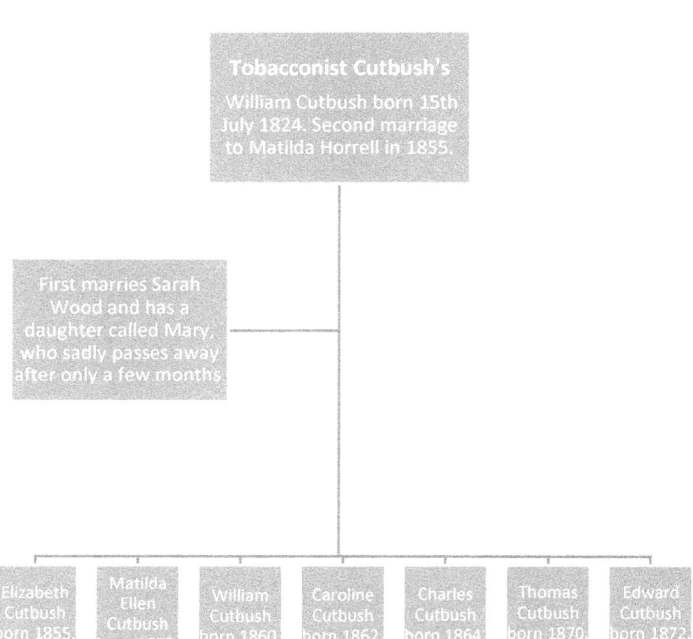

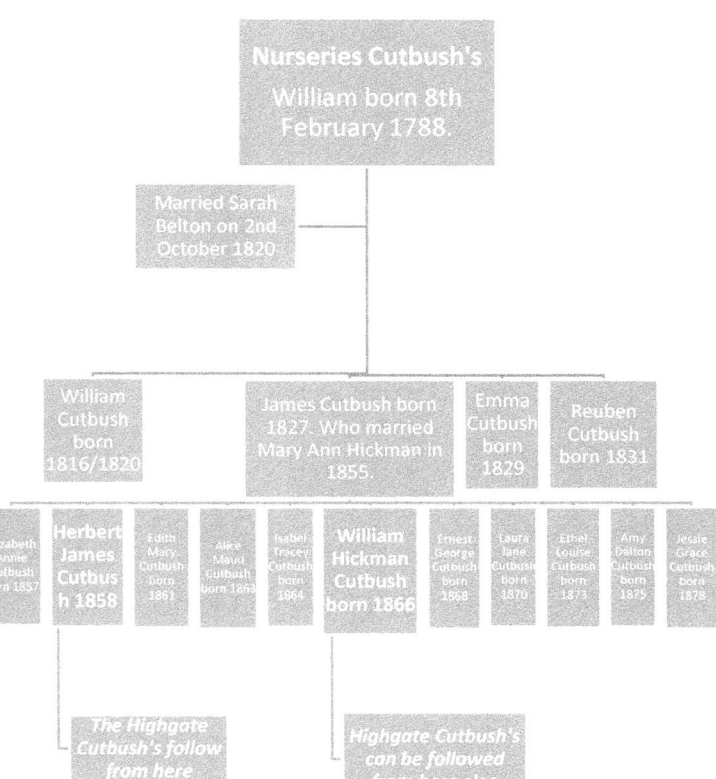

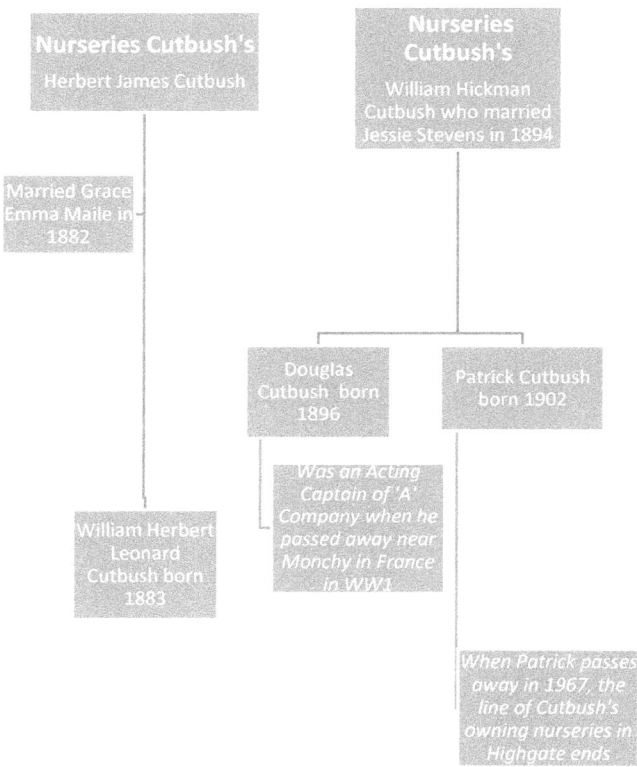

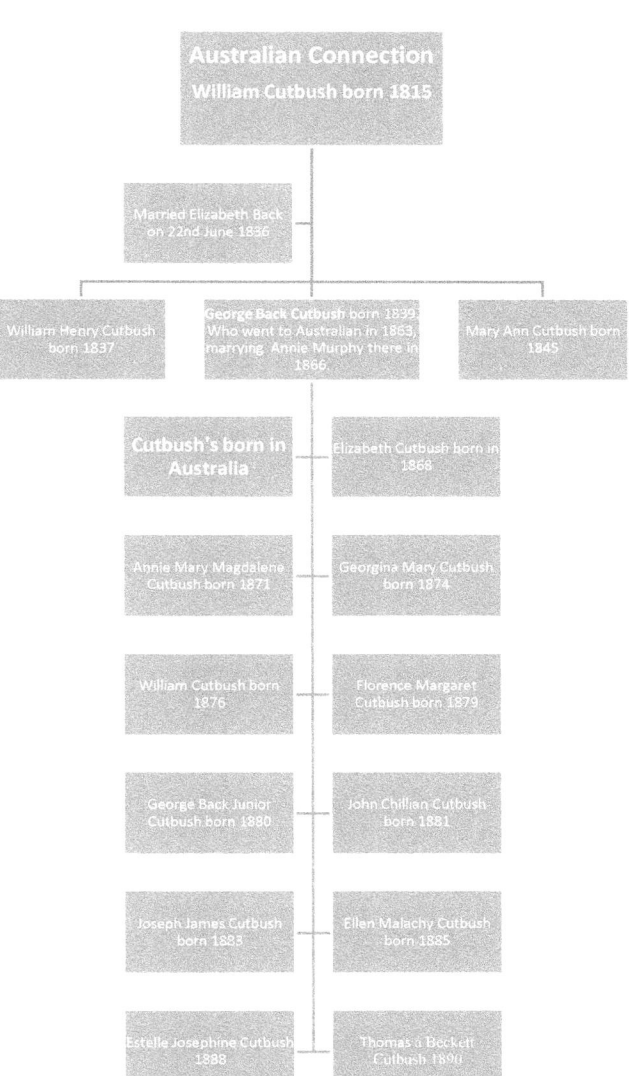

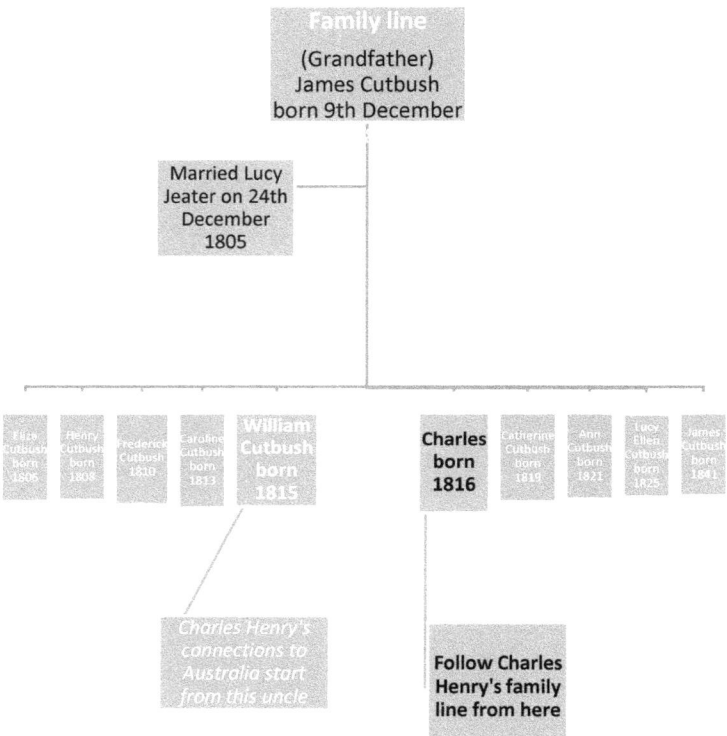

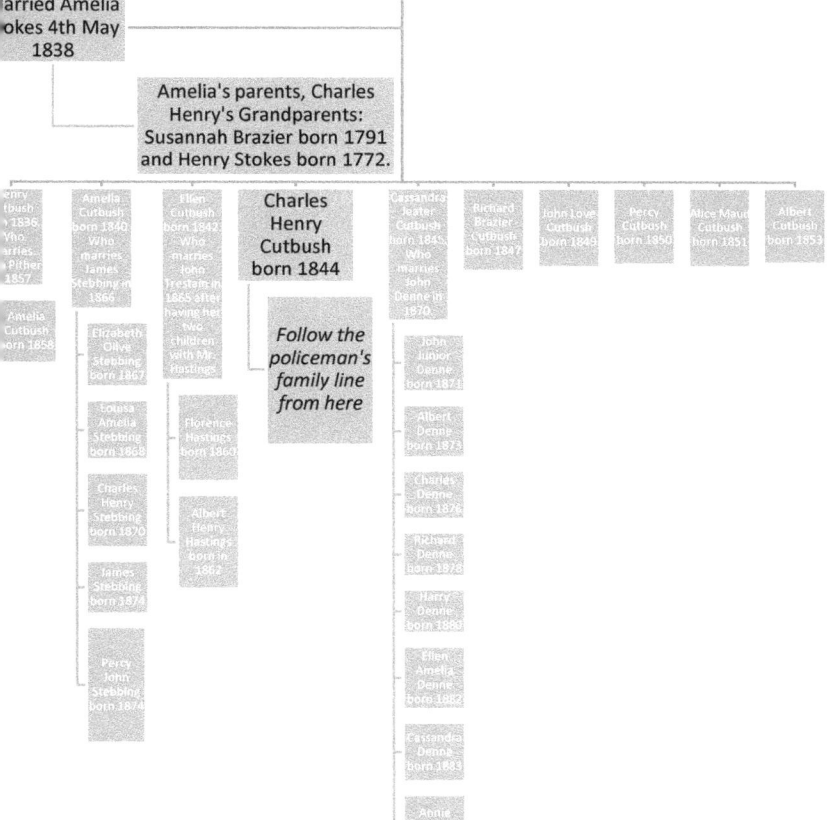

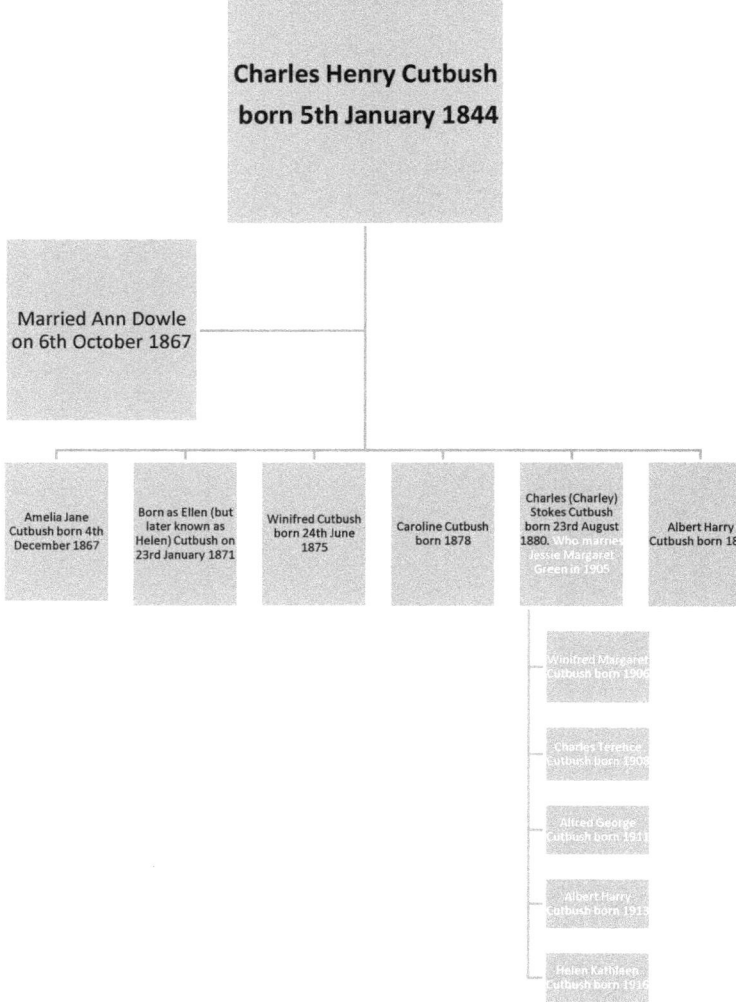

Looking into the eyes...

The author *could* end the book there, as we have already gone into the lives of Charles Henry's children and *their* children earlier in this book.

However, ending on Charles Henry's passing didn't seem quite right to the author, *it isn't exactly a positive note to end on, is it?*

So, the author has chosen to actually end on a moment that had an important and profound effect on her as she researched this book...

The author has been lucky enough to have been in contact with a few members of the living day Cutbush family, from various different branches of that very vast family tree.

Through them, she was even luckier to have seen family photographs of some of the major characters within this book.

Sadly, it was suggested to the author that other members of the family might not be happy with having the photographs being reproduced in a book.

Which of course, the author respects fully, and she would never wish to upset any family member. Even ones she has not met before.

However, what the author will try her best to do, is to describe these photographs, so that the reader has a closer connection to every piece of research the author has seen[636].

...

Amelia Cutbush, Charles Henry's mother's photograph depicts her in her older life, perhaps at the time when she was living with her son at Number 3 Burnley Road, Stockwell.

She wears a laced cap of a dark colour, with lace curls falling down at the back of the head to her shoulders. As the part of her hair that is on show in the photograph, is a lighter colour than the lace, she could have had blonde or perhaps she had light brown hair, which seems to be straight without curls.

The cap, seems to make her look as if she has a large forehead, but without the cap this might not have been the case.

Her eyebrows are not hugely highlighted in the black and white photograph, which does indicate blonde or perhaps light brown hair too, her eyes are hooded and the nose is long and curled up at the end.

Her mouth is small, with the top lip hardly on show and she has a rounded chin to match her rounded face.

In the photograph she is wearing a large dark lace choker with some sort of brooch in the middle, she is wearing a

---

[636] The author would like to thank the family members she has been in contact with, that would like to remain private and not to have their names published, to allow her to see these photographs.

dark shawl across her shoulders with what looks like a silk dress with a large bow underneath.

Ellen Trestain nee Cutbush, Charles Henry's older sister's photograph captures her in middle age. Her pose is interesting because she is not just sitting on a chair looking at the camera, she is leaning towards a wooden desk with her right arm resting upon a book on that desk.

Her hair is brushed back and seems to be quite long, possibly in a brown colour and straight. Her facial features, seems to be very much like her mother's features, with the same hooded eyes and same shaped nose.

She has a pair of long earrings on, with rings on her right hand, the right wrist also seems to have a pearl bracelet surrounding it. On the left hand is a wedding ring, which helps to date the photograph a little better as she does not marry until 1st April 1865, when she was twenty three years old.

Her dress seems formal and of good quality with many layers of silk and lace detailing. She appears to have been very healthy and her pose suggests someone that is very confident, perhaps even little forceful.

Cassandra Denne nee Cutbush, Charles Henry's younger sister's photograph again depicts her in middle age. At the bottom of the photograph it states 'F. Bailey. Canterbury' which helps to date the photograph as we know that after she marries, she moves and spends the rest of her life in Canterbury, eventually being buried there in Canterbury City Cemetery.

She, like her sister seems to be very healthy in size and the nose and mouth is like her mother's, however her eyes don't seem to be the same, although they are deep set they don't seem to be as hooded as both are sister's eyes and mother's eyes were.

Her long hair is clip up and parted in the middle, the colour is very light to make us feel when looking at it, that she is blonde.

Her dress looks very expensive for the time, the top shawl, which looks to be a part of the dress, seems to look like it is made of sequins, while the rest of the dress is a dark silk.

She wears two brooches, one at the collar of the dress, of a lighter colour and one a little further down the dress of a darker colour, with an added chained necklace.

...

Amelia Cutbush, Charles Henry's oldest sister has been shown to the author in a number of different photographs as already mentioned in this book. However, there is another photograph that shows her features more clearly, which the author will try to describe now.

She is almost the spitting image of her mother, just perhaps with darker hair, it certainly feels like we are looking at the same woman.

Her dress again is of a dark colour with a high-necked collar, made of silk. She wears her dress with a long-chained necklace, like her sister, but added with it is a large brooch that seems to have a locket pendant hanging from it.

The author has even been able to see photographs of **William and Elizabeth Cutbush**, Charles Henry's uncle that lived out his retirement and was buried in Hythe in Kent, with one of his sons and wife.

One photograph of William, shows him in his bed in later years but in the other photograph he and his wife are posing for it. Elizabeth is sitting down on a chair while William stands beside her with a walking stick.

Elizabeth seems to have greying hair clipped back into a white hat with a dark brim and dark ribbon, she wears spectacles with a thin frame and seems to be almost smiling.

Her dress seems dull and of a rough material being dark with a buttoned-up front and a brooch at the collar. She is holding, what looks like to be a pair of gloves.

William has the overall look of a Victorian shop keeper, he has thinning hair but with brushy eyebrows and a beard to match, which covers his mouth.

His long dark coat reaches to just above his knees, with a pair of dark trousered legs standing in a pair of leather shoes at the bottom of the coat. It certainly seems as if this couple were wearing their 'Sunday best' for this photograph.

The author has also seen a photograph of William's son, so Charles Henry's cousin, **George Back Cutbush**. He was the man that went to and stayed in Australia.

He looks very much a business man with means, he sits on a chair looking comfortably at the camera. He has white thinning hair with a full white beard and linking moustache, making it hard to see his actual mouth.

His nose seems large and his eyes are curved in shape to make them look like they are almost smiling. He wears a coat that is slightly unbuttoned to show a waist coat with an Albert Chain.

Then, there is **Douglas Cutbush**, the soldier that died in battle. The photograph of him that the author has seen is the one that was sent to his father, when news broke that Douglas had died, as mentioned already in this book.

He is wearing his army uniform with a cap, he is looking straight at the camera, with a hard stare, his eyes are rounded and not hooded.

His nose is long and curled at the end, with a larger bottom lip to the top one that also has the starting of a moustache laying above it.

…

Finally, we turn to **Charles Henry Cutbush**, himself. To have actually seen a photograph of the main player within this book was so wonderful and something the author thought she would never be able to see.

To *look into the eyes* of the man we have been researching, to wonder what he was thinking at the time of the photograph and if he ever knew what was to become of him, meant so much to the author.

Charles Henry looks very young in the photograph, around his twenties, suggesting the photograph could have been taken at the time when he had just married and joined the Metropolitan Police force.

He is sitting on a chair looking away from the camera. His dark hair is trimmed short but with lots of volume, his ears are slightly pointed at the top and rounded at the bottom and his eyebrows are dark and slightly pointed inwards from the nose end.

His eyes are slightly hooded but not has much as his mother's eyes and are very, very dark in colour, he stares to his left, strongly and with purpose.

His nose is not as long as his mother's but is rounded at the end like hers, his mouth has equalled sized bottom and top lips and they almost stand out a bit from his face, his overall face is rounded at the top and pointed at the bottom.

He wears a basic suit at the time, with a waistcoat and dark bow tie and there is a slight suggestion of a wedding band on his finger.

...

Finally, the author has in her collection one more image, that over the time she has researched this book it has become very important to her and to the aim of what she is trying to do in this series of book about policemen that had some involvement in the Jack the Ripper case of 1888, that she thought she would share it with you, the reader.

It is a postcard that the author has carried around with her as she travelled to all the places she has been to for the research of this book.

It is a postcard that has been said to be dated around the turn of the century, possibly a couple of years after the passing of Charles Henry Cutbush.

It shows a quiet street, with trees lining the route on one side. There are only a few people within the postcard walking along the street, one of them, ironically perhaps, is a policeman.

On the other side of the road to the trees, is a prominent building, its spire reaches high up to the clear blue sky, this is St Michael's Church in Stockwell Park Road…

We will probably never know or find enough evidence to prove where Charles Henry was buried or had his ashes scattered because of the way he passed on.

However, the author can't just leave it there for Charles Henry Cutbush.

She may not be able to help get him a headstone, like she is trying to do with Inspector Edmund John James Reid[637]. The same Edmund Reid that has been mentioned a few times in this book.

However, she still wanted to do something for Charles Henry, something that perhaps may seem small to some but something the author just had to do.

This is because, for the author, writing about these lives, these pieces of history, means more to her than the task itself.

---

[637] Working with the Herne Bay Cemetery staff.

She really does care for everyone of those lives, just as much as she cares about future generations, from whatever background, for whatever reason, that are reading about the people that were a part of history, because they are important to help to keep history alive too.

So that is why she took the postcard everywhere with her and every time she looked at it she couldn't help but wonder what if Charles Henry Cutbush's last resting place, is the place within this postcard?

Was Charles Henry's last resting place within a church, that as we now know has its own tales of suicide and a church that more than likely was Charles Henry's place to visit on a Sunday morning?

For that possibility no matter how slim and maybe because of the meaning behind her own actions, this postcard has even more meaning, for Charles Henry's story. Whether he is actually within the church's grounds or not. Who knows? Who can really say?

The postcard of St Michael's Church, Stockwell Park Road from the author's collection.

However, the author would like to remember Charles Henry Cutbush as he was in the portrait photograph she has just described.

When he was simply a son, a husband and perhaps knowing he will be a father, very soon.

When Charles Henry Cutbush was the innocent and strong, young man before all the troubles and problems, before all the stories and suggestions, before all the cases and inquiries and before we knew, that he would be *somewhere without a headstone*.

This is because the photograph she has described is. in her eyes at least, a positive one and for that reason alone is why the author hopes the reader will agree with her, *to end with that picture in our heads is the nicest way to end this book and the story of Superintendent Charles Henry Cutbush.*

These series of books of the lives behind Victorian crimes will continue…

Forget me not…

About the Author

Amanda Harvey Purse has studied the Jack the Ripper case for over twenty five years, she became a tour guide and historical researcher for the City of London Police Museum ten years ago.

Through this museum she has helped many television programmes and documentaries for the BBC, ITV, Channel 4, and The History Channel, on a whole range of different of different topics from the Victorian era and the monarchy, to the Tudors and King Richard III, while also occasionally dealing with the Ruth Ellis case, Richardson's and the Krays and even the suffragettes.

She is a member of the Metropolitan Police Historical Society and has written many articles for magazines, such as The True Crime Dagger, The Whitechapel Society Journal and The Ripperologist.

Amanda is the author behind, Jack the Ripper's Many Faces, Dead Bodies Do Tell Tales, The Strange Case of Caroline Maxwell, The Adventures of Amelia Christie, Binky the Tabby Cat Tails and Victorian Lives behind Victorian Crimes.

...

In her series of books about the lives of the policemen who had some involvement in the Jack the Ripper case of 1888, she has written:

Jack and Old Jewry: The City of London Policemen Who Hunted the Ripper – This book covers the lives of about thirty policemen and the three doctors who was in attendance at the only suggested Jack the Ripper murder than happened in the City of London, while also mentioning the life of Catherine Eddowes, who sadly passed away there.

Inspector Reid: The Real Ripper Street – This book covers the life of Inspector Edmund John James Reid and family and while as the cases he worked on. The only two aims of this book, is to highlight the need for Edmund to have a headstone and to raise funds to get that headstone.

The Cutbush Connections: In Flowers, In Blood and In the Ripper case is her third book in this series.

Lightning Source UK Ltd.
Milton Keynes UK
UKHW040712220419
341411UK00001B/40/P